Purple Crayon Confidence:
A Strategic Workbook to Build and Maintain Self-Assurance

Kayla-Leah Rich

WIPublish

Purple Crayon Confidence
© 2017 by Kayla-Leah Rich
www.kayla-leah.com

Published by WIPublish
A Division of Women Ignite International
Boise, ID
www.womenigniteidaho.com

TABLE OF CONTENTS

DEDICATION

It takes dedication to roll with me!

I am grateful to my ever-supportive husband, Jason, who has always believed I could do anything I set my mind to. He has endured many Dr. Pepper powered writing sessions. I am so glad I don't have to convince you to come along with me on all my ideas. Thank you for partnering with me on this crazy journey called life.

To our four boys, Parker, Rider, Carter, and Porter. Thank you for tolerating the ride so well.

To my parents, Ron and Ramona, thank you for helping me build a foundation of confidence that has brought me such great joy.

ACKNOWLEDGMENTS

I am grateful for the work and encouragement of my editor, Amy Beck. Thanks for loving this book along with me.

I am indebted to Terilee Harrison of WIPublish for her support and expertise.

I am grateful for some dear friends and family in my life who helped shape the confident person I am today: Ciera Bench, Jessica Fenton, Ashley Holt, Amy Robinson, Mary Sandhal, Zetta Simpson, Melanie Shreeve, and Laura Sonderegger, and my Zena Tribe.

Lastly (mainly to freak her out, thinking I forgot her), my sister Kelsey. Thank you for encouraging me to do what I love, and having no doubt that I could do it.

FOREWORD

Kayla's book is such a timely, powerful resource!

We exist in a world where the news media, digital platforms, and too often, our own networks point out our flaws, or misunderstand us. And, we often don't get our own selves! **Confidence** *is truly one of the keys to sustainable success in life, business and relationships.* **Purple Crayon Confidence** is just the right mix of stories, strategies, practical applications, exercises, and the motivation to get growing!

Kayla is a successful Entrepreneur, Humanitarian and Life Coach. She is the same amazing woman on and off the stage, in her home in Idaho, or on the ground serving in Haiti. She continues to work on her own growth, while selflessly helping others to embrace themselves, and their abilities and goals. Her combination of inspiration and tools will be magical for anyone truly wanting to grow, be honest about where they are, and those who do the work with her easy to implement guide.

In my experience as a longtime Entrepreneur, Speaker, Coach/Consultant in business and human development, *confidence is one of the number one things that can hold anyone back from scaling in every area of life.* The good news is, it's so attainable to expand your compelling confidence, and exponentially grow your success, fulfillment and sustainability at work, and in your life. This book is one of the best ways I have seen to do just that.

What are you waiting for? Your future is getting excited, even now, as you take your next steps.

Sheli G
SheliG.com
Speaker | Business Consultant | Team Igniter | Comedian
CEO Women Ignite International

INTRODUCTION

I see you. Even though part of you doesn't want to be seen, I see you. I would write your name, but I don't want to put you on the spot. I see you feeling insignificant, insecure, unworthy, invisible.

I see you.

I see that you are beat up from what life has dished out. I see you are tired, struggling to want to fight the fight another day.

Hiding does have its comfort.

Besides, you may rationalize, you don't have much to offer.

But I see you. I see the amazing you, shrinking away from filling the full measure of your creation. I see you and my insides ache for you. I want so bad, almost enough for both of us, for you to see the teensiest glimpse of who you really are, the power, and brilliance and you-ness that you are hiding inside you.

I would think you selfish. Selfish for shrinking, selfish for hiding all your amazingness, for not sharing with the world the flavor that only you can bring. For holding back, denying us of your best self. But that wouldn't be right. I know your intention isn't to be selfish, though selfishness is the result. You are keeping all your wonderfulness to yourself. But I worry that even you don't enjoy you.

I am writing this book, with all the best tools and tips I have seen work, in hopes that maybe there is something here that can convince you that it isn't too late. That living a life of confidence can bring great joy to you and to the world. When you show up as you, then there is no limit to what can happen. I see you, I see your struggle, and in spite of it I am inviting you to see yourself with new eyes.

I hope to share with you in these pages some practices and principles that have been proven to develop and increase self-confidence. This workbook is designed to evoke self-reflection. Each chapter includes principles of self-confidence with some suggested practices on how to develop and maintain a healthy sense of self. Each chapter stands individually, however, combined I hope to help you increase your confidence by degrees. I believe confidence is a process, but I also believe you can progress by leaps and bounds by making a focused effort.

There are a few things that may appear at the end of some chapters that I would like to explain.

"In Other(s) Words"

This is a grouping of quotes from other authorities on the topics of the chapter. I have added quotes after the chapter to help you continue to ponder on what was learned. I think when we hear several "witnesses" of the same principle it solidifies what we have are being taught.. Feel free to add your own at the end of each chapter. This could be a lovely place to collect powerful words that can remind you of your wonderfulness.

"Helping Others" *Fill their buckets!.*

These are tips on how you might help others around you apply the principles of the chapter, perhaps it is a parent, sibling, child, or friend whom you want to help grow in confidence. Of course, my hope would be that they would read this book themselves, but if it isn't the right time for them, these tips can help you to help them. I also believe when you teach someone a principle you are learning it helps the principle become a part of you. I encourage you to help others while you work on your own confidence.

"Insight of God"

A section of wisdom gained from the Bible on confidence. I have separated this out for those whose belief system may not align with mine. However, the depth I feel it adds to this discussion could not be left out. To me it is insight from God, or how we are viewed in the sight of God.

"Ed(you)cation"

This is your homework. These exercises are designed to develop and maintain confidence, a chance to get to know "you" better. Take time to do the suggested exercises. You can easily skip over them, assuming you understand the purpose of the exercises and therefore don't need to do them. However, there is a difference in understanding an exercise and actually doing it. I understand the power of push-ups, but I receive no benefit from this power until I actually do push-ups.

"Journal Pages"

Journaling as you read this book has great benefits. Writing allows you to get feelings and thoughts out of you and into reality. Feel free to mark up the pages, circle, highlight, cross out, and write notes to yourself in all the blank spaces.

I hope that this book can remind you of what you have forgotten about yourself, or teach you something you did not yet know. When you show up as you, then there is no limit to what can happen. I have seen these principles and practices transform lives. I have seen the world benefit from the change within someone who is filling the measure of their creation.

I also see you, I see your struggle, and, in spite of it all, I am inviting you to see yourself with new eyes.

Helping Others

Take the time to stop and really look someone in the eyes. Acknowledge the good things you see in them. Maybe even say, "You may not be comfortable hearing this, so you don't really need to reply, but I really admire _____." Be liberal with your heartfelt compliments of others around you. We hear so many negative messages in media and in our own heads; a positive compliment goes a long way!

In Other(s) Words

Your need for acceptance can make you invisible in this world.
Don't let anything stand in the way of the light that shines
through this form. Risk being seen in all of your glory.
— Jim Carrey (1)

Insight of God

In the New Testament, Matthew 5:13-16 reads:

Ye are the salt of the earth: but if the salt has lost his savour,
wherewith shall it be salted? It is thenceforth good for nothing, but to
be cast out, and to be trodden under foot of men.

Ye are the light of the world. A city that is set on a hill cannot be hid.

Neither do men light a candle, and put it under a bushel, but on a
candlestick; and it giveth light unto all that are in the house.

Let your light so shine before men, that they may see your good
works, and glorify your Father which is in heaven. (2)

In these verses, Matthew records three examples of how we ought
to be.

Perhaps, in this day and age, we are not familiar with how essential
salt is and has been through history. Salt preserves meats, which was
vital in Matthew's time when refrigeration was not available. Salt is
essential to sustain life, not just for preserving meats for food but
because of the crucial role it plays in our bodies at the cellular level, and
as it affects the cardiovascular and nervous system. We literally would
die without salt. So if salt has lost its savour, then it has lost its essence,
its life preserving qualities.

Sometimes we may feel like we have lost our savour, that we are
good for nothing. It is the adversary who wants us to feel like this way,
for he wants us to feel trodden underfoot. These verses of the Bible
remind us of how important we are. They remind us to not hide our
light, to not diminish or shrink but shine like a city on a hill or a candle
in the darkness.

I love the words from Marianne Williamson as she reminds us to let our light shine:

"Our deepest fear is not that we are inadequate. Our deepest fear is that we are powerful beyond measure. It is our light, not our darkness that most frightens us. We ask ourselves, Who am I to be brilliant, gorgeous, talented, fabulous? Actually, who are you not to be? You are a child of God. Your playing small does not serve the world. There is nothing enlightened about shrinking so that other people won't feel insecure around you. We are all meant to shine, as children do. We were born to make manifest the glory of God that is within us. It's not just in some of us; it's in everyone. And as we let our own light shine, we unconsciously give other people permission to do the same. As we are liberated from our own fear, our presence automatically liberates others."

-- Marianne Williamson (3)

You are the salt, you are the light, and you are the candle. When you let your light shine, that light allows others to glorify our Father in Heaven. It may seem easier to hide, to diminish the light within us. But God is calling us to do more.

Ed(you)cation

Commit to doing the exercises in this book. Commit to recording your feelings at the end of each chapter in a journal or in the margins. Record the things you are doing well. Record the things that have been a struggle. Your homework is to write down your feelings after reading the introduction.

I will take this book to heart & try with all my might to learn and grow from it.

I want to be a confident woman!

"Self-confidence is the first requisite to great undertakings."
- Samuel Johnson

FOUNDATION OF CONFIDENCE

I love Idaho. We have our own little slice of heaven here on our two-and-a-half acres, raising chickens, sticks, dirt and boys. We have no desire to ever leave. However, during a time when my husband, Jason, worked out-of-state, the boys and I were prompted to join him for a six-month stint. I found a perfect rental home just fifteen minutes from the beach in Corpus Christi, Texas. Idaho is awesome, but hanging out at the beach every weekend is not a bad tradeoff.

Reading over my rental agreement, I came across something I had never heard of before. As the renter, I would be contractually obligated to water the foundation regularly. What? Water the foundation? I had no idea what the landlord was referring to, so I called her for some clarification.

What I learned was that the soil in that part of Texas has a high clay content. The extremes in weather conditions cause the soil to expand and contract drastically. With expanding soil, foundations become cracked and broken, so to avoid damage it is imperative that the soil around the foundation be regularly watered. With my new insight, I signed on the dotted line, prepared to water the foundation faithfully.

I was surprised that in the short time we lived in the rental house on that quiet street, four of my neighbors had to have extensive repairs done to their foundations. To restore the foundation, cylinders of concrete were placed beneath the house to support sagging, shifting footings. In extreme cases, the house had to be hoisted up and the entire foundation replaced. Such extreme efforts are undoubtedly expensive and time-consuming.

I find the effect clay levels in the Texas soil can have on concrete structures fascinating. More importantly, though, are the parallels that can be drawn between these foundations and our self-confidence.

Like foundations, confidence supports you in many areas: work, relationships, how you view yourself, and even how you view the world around you. Your life is built on how you feel about yourself. As I found in Texas, even the sturdiest and properly built foundations will crack and break up if not properly maintained as the soil around them shifts.

Our foundation of confidence is developed in our childhood

How we are parented greatly affects our self-view. Parents who are critical and demanding can leave a child feeling wrong or unworthy of love. The voice of the parent inside a child's head is very loud, often becoming the voice of their self-thought. Even well meaning, overprotective parents can rob a child of opportunities for self-reliance and the confidence building feeling of accomplishment.

If this is the type of parenting you experienced as a child, there is hope yet for your confidence! Because confidence is a learned skill, it can still be learned no matter how you were raised.

"Low self-confidence isn't a life sentence. Self-confidence can be learned, practiced, and mastered--just like any other skill, once you master it, everything in your life will change for the better."
– Barrie Davenport (4)

We have the ability to do our own groundwork. If you are repairing your confidence foundation as an adult, you are not alone. We all have to create our own life to one degree or another building on what was passed on to us.

"People often say that this or that person has not yet found himself. But the self is not something one finds, it is something one creates."
— Thomas Szasz

Parents who are accepting and who express confidence in a child's abilities start the early groundwork for their children to build their own self-assurance. Parents who provide opportunities for self-reliance add to this groundwork. This is an advantage for sure, however, the work is not done, as I learned with our Texas foundation. Confidence isn't a crock-pot, a "set it and forget it" thing. Because our world is constantly shifting--jobs, relationships, responsibilities, roles--if we are not watering our foundations or maintaining our confidence to counter these shifts, we will feel shaky at best and at worst find ourselves in need of a complete overhaul.

Our confidence can be affected by the following changes like the expanding and contracting soil.

Relationships:

• Dating, with its ups and downs, can be rough on self-esteem. It can be difficult to second guess how strangers feel about us, and even more difficult if we feel rejected.

• Marriage is a constantly moving and growing relationship, there are many adjustments to be made through the years that can have an effect on how self-assured you are.

• Relationships with siblings, parents, and in-laws can put strains on self-worth.

• Friendships formed in the office, in the neighborhood, or with hobbies/interests can fluctuate and cause shifts in self-confidence.

Moving:

I have moved around the block and across the country. I have moved to new places and moved back to old places. Moving has a way of shifting your footing. There are so many factors that come with a move! Moving affects employment and sometimes it limits access to previous friendships. Changing where you live can be complicated as a parent when you are addressing your own feelings during a move and trying to ease the feelings of your offspring as well. Moving is sometimes accompanied with fear and some moves have higher stakes. All these factors make moving a big confidence shifter.

Employment:

Searching for new employment with resumes, interviews, rejections, and acceptances can all affect feelings of self-worth. In a different job the adjustments to new information and systems can leave even the smartest candidate feeling a little befuddled. Even with regular employment changes in leadership, co-workers or procedures can shake a foundation.

Body Changes:

- Weight fluctuation
- Skin changes
- Aging
- Acne
- Wrinkles
- Receding hairlines
- Vision issues

so much yes

I could go on and on about our bodies. These sometimes drastic changes can leave us feeling like we are having an out-of-body experience. Maybe at some level we know that we are more than our body, however, physical changes can affect how we view ourselves.

Health:

Whether the challenges in health are your own or in someone in your circle, the changes will affect your foundation of self-confidence. Health seems to put things in perspective. If a co-worker or high school friend has a heart attack, it tends to cause us to evaluate our priorities and where we are in our life. When we have health issues that limit us, we can start to question our worth. Having a child or parent with health problems often require us to learn new things which present challenges to our abilities..

18

Parenting:

Even trying to conceive a child can affect confidence. For those who struggle with fertility, feelings of brokenness and unworthiness are strong. If hormones are used to increase likelihood of conception, the physical effects it has on the body are confidence-shifting.

For those who experience pregnancy, the changes are daunting.

Those going through the rigors of adoption can at times be plagued with self-doubts.

Preparing for parenthood can feel overwhelming as we assess our ability to care for another human being.

As amazing as it is to add to your family, it does change the relationships of those who welcome the child. There is now another person to provide for, another person's feelings to consider. And although love multiplies, some things get divided, like time, space, and energy. This is why, even with subsequent children, foundations of self-confidence can shift.

Then when your child moves out of one phase and into the next (just when you thought you had that last phase figured out!) changes can rock the boat again. Even having a child leave the nest can cause a shift in life.

As you can see, there are many things that can affect the groundwork we build our confidence upon or shift our foundations over the years. I highlight these changes for you, not to discourage, but to validate life situations you may have encountered over the years that can have affected your feelings of self-worth.

The good news is there are specific habits you can develop that can build and expand your confidence. To some readers, this book represents watering the soil so the foundation won't crack. To others it looks more like we are hoisting up the house to put in the cement cylinders, and to some it is a complete overhaul where the house is lifted, the previously crumbling foundation removed, the ground prepared, the foundation rebuilt surer and stronger than ever.

It is never too late, and it is worth every effort! The side effects of having self-confidence are amazing.

"If we all did the things we are capable of doing, we would literally astound ourselves."
-Thomas Alva Edison

I have been able to examine in-depth what having confidence has done for my life and how my confidence has affected my section of the world. Here are some snap-shots of the result of my self-confidence.

Confidence has allowed me to say "YES" to new opportunities.

My friend posted once on social media that she was going to Haiti to volunteer in medical clinics, and she opened the invitation to anyone who wanted to come along. My response was immediate--I knew I had to go. The idea scared me, but I knew I had to do it. I said yes because of my self-assurance.

When that friend was unable to go to Haiti because of a major health battle (cancer is awful), I chose to say "YES" again to going to Haiti all by myself. This was a "yes" to new foods (a very big concern since I am a plain meat and potatoes gal), a new culture, and international travel. It meant I would arrive by myself in a foreign country at night without the ability to easily communicate since I did not speak Creole.

My "yes" afforded me one of the most poignant experiences in my life. That trip, and my later return to Haiti, changed me and my heart in ways that I can't even articulate. It expanded my worldview, gave depth to my life's purpose, increased my gratitude, broke my heart and healed it again.

Another "Yes" opportunity came when I heard they were taking applications to speak on the TED stage, I did not hesitate to throw my name in the hat. I submitted application materials and pitched my idea for this phenomenal opportunity because of my foundation of self-confidence. Every part of the TED experience requires confidence, from applying to stepping on that red dot and spreading your idea. I have dreamed of speaking in this very setting since I saw my very first

first TED talk. I am excited that a TED talk is now part of my life story. There is something soul invigorating about accomplishing such a "bucket list" item.

Confidence allows me to be a part of something bigger than myself.

I set out to start a chapter of a non-profit called Days For Girls with the goal of taking 1000 hand-made reusable feminine hygiene kits to the girls of Haiti before I even laid eyes on a kit. I knew the kits would give girls more worry free period days at school and women more days at work.

I did not know how to run a non-profit chapter of this organization. I did not know how I was going to fit it into my life. I decided I would figure out each piece as I went along. I was okay taking a few steps in the dark knowing that illumination would come.

The work was fast and furious, but I was able to reach my goals and returned with kits for Haiti within eight months of starting my chapter.

I also involved over 600 volunteers, organized and executed over twenty events, built a board of willing volunteers, and returned to Haiti with a team for classes and distribution.

Helping get appropriate feminine hygiene supplies to "Every girl. Everywhere. Period." is bigger than I am, but confidence allows me to jump in with both feet and see what I can do.

(For more information about this great organization go to daysforgirls.org.)

Confidence allows me to advocate for myself and for others.

As a mom, you want the best for your children. One of my boys had been struggling at school for years and was so unhappy, part of trying to figure out the combination for his happiness was an evaluation that resulted in a diagnosis of Autism. I was trying to learn all that I could about this Asperger's diagnosis for my son, I realized that I was called to be his advocate in all situations. At church, at school, at the doctor's office--I would need to be his voice. It required confidence to be able to ask the right questions, insist on the right treatments, and go to bat for my son time and again. I always felt like his little spirit was bigger than his body, and it was my job to make sure no one else squashed him. It doesn't come naturally to stand up to "experts," but self-assurance helps me to follow my gut, even when it conflicted with expert opinions.

In this world where so many people are left without a voice, confidence allows you to be their voice when necessary.

I am able to advocate for myself in a variety of circumstances and relationships. I can think of situations as a consumer, a patient, a spouse, sibling, or as a friend where I have had to ask for (or sometimes demand) what I need. Without a sure foundation, it would be easy to feel as though we have no say in the things affecting our lives. Confidence gives you a voice.

Here are some other noted benefits. Self-Confidence helps you:

Manage fear.
Maintain a positive attitude.
Increase performance.
Have more happiness.
Have better relationships.
Feel more connected.
Influence others.
Control emotions, behaviors.
Have social ease.
Sleep better.
Withstand peer pressure.
Articulate your views.
Have a greater sense of worth.
Have freedom from doubt.
Have peace of mind.
Achieve greater success.
Increase job opportunities.
Attract others.
Develop resilience.

Holding my head up, my shoulders back, a smile on my face, and a twinkle in my eye is what confidence looks like on me. Within me confidence fills me with possibilities, growth, fulfillment, and joy. Developing your foundation is a worthwhile pursuit at any age, worthy of building our lives upon. Within these chapters, you will find tools to help you build and maintain a sure foundation of confidence.

In Other(s) Words

"Once we believe in ourselves, we can risk curiosity, wonder, spontaneous delight, or any experience that reveals the human spirit."
-e.e. Cummings

"You have brains in your head. You have feet in your shoes.
You can steer yourself in any direction you choose.
You're on your own. And you know what you know.
You are the guy who'll decide where to go."
-Dr. Seuss (5)

Insight of God

In the New Testament, we are given this parable:
Therefore, whosoever heareth these sayings of mine, and doeth them, I will liken him unto a wise man, which built his house upon a rock: And the rain descended, and the floods came, and the winds blew, and beat upon that house; and it fell not: for it was founded upon a rock. And every one that heareth these sayings of mine, and doeth them not, shall be likened unto a foolish man, which built his house upon the sand: And the rain descended, and the floods came, and the winds blew, and beat upon that house; and it fell: and great was the fall of it. (Matt. 7:24-27)

Our confidence is much like this parable. We need to build on a rock—a sure foundation. We are building our confidence on the rock of whom God knows we are and who we can become through Him. When we build our confidence on Him, come what may, whether winds, rains, or floods, we will not fall.

I am a daughter of God!

4 my foundation!

23

Helping Others

If you interact with children as a teacher, relative or parent, you have the opportunity to help them build a foundation of self-confidence. You can share confidence in their abilities, give opportunities for self-reliance, and celebrate their accomplishments.

Ed(you)cation

Ponder the following questions:
- Did your parents prepare a groundwork for your confidence?
- Did you have to prepare your own footings?
- Are you a confident person?
- On a scale of 1-10 how confident are you?
  1 2 3 4 5 6 7 8 9 10
- When do you feel the most confident?
- When do you feel the least confident?
- From the list of life changes above, underline the life changes you have experienced thus far.
- Who in your life seems to exhibit self-confidence?
- What affect does this confidence seem to have on their life?
- What benefits of confidence do you want to see in your life?

I think I had a lot of confidence as a child.
Teenagehood sorta threw some of that out
the window. I think learning my worth as a
child of God really helped a lot.

I believe that overall, I am a confident person,
but certain times much of it is forgotten for a
short time.

I have the most confidence around certain
friends and in situations where I have some
role of leadership. I am very confident when
I am leading an FPU class or when I'm
teaching a lesson in Relief Society. However,
in the time leading up to those moments, I am
nervous and not confident in my abilities.

I think the only one of those life changes that
does NOT apply to me is health.

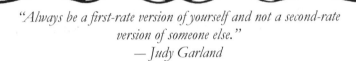

"Always be a first-rate version of yourself and not a second-rate version of someone else."
— Judy Garland

KINDERGARTEN WISDOM

Kindergarten was such a magical time for me; there were so many new experiences every day.

On my first day of school, my dad took me to the wrong classroom. I really liked it there. We sat on a big rug while the teacher played the piano and we sang, "B-I-N-G-O! B-I-N-G-O! B-I-N-G-O! And Bingo was his name-o!" I think we made it through about three songs before my real teacher came and took me away to a piano-less classroom. We had a tape player.

Even right now, the sight, sounds, and flavors of kindergarten are tickling my memory: the plastic crates that held milk for our snacks, nap time on the carpet, not to mention getting sent to the corner when I stood my pencil up vertically (that's right, I was a total rebel). I also remember getting sick when I was forced to eat my banana, and then hiding my banana in my milk carton from that time forward. To this day, the smell of bananas makes me nauseous. I still feed them to my kiddos because I know they are good for them, but I wage an internal struggle every time they eat them.

One of my favorite activities in kindergarten was coloring. We sat at long rectangular tables and shared coffee cans filled with big, fat crayons. With five other siblings at my house, crayons were frequently broken or lost altogether. I had never seen big crayons before.

I loved to color. Purple was my favorite color at the time. Each day, I would grab my purple crayon and color a masterpiece. I was pretty happy until one day I noticed that everyone at my table was trying to get the gray crayon. Some kids would even sit and wait for the gray crayon. I didn't understand what was so cool about gray. In my opinion, gray wasn't even a color. It was so boring compared to vibrant purple. After observing for a while, I realized that everyone wanted gray because it was the most like silver. Almost all the kids vied for the gray crayon. Soon, I too, would wait for the gray. I stopped using purple.

We learn how to be in this world by watching others. As babies, we learn to walk and talk and mimic our parents. It is so great to learn this way. Even as we go to school we watch to see where to hang our coats or how to sit crisscross applesauce on the rug (all very important things). There is nothing wrong with learning how to navigate this world by watching others.

That is, until you get *Gray Crayon Syndrome*--when you leave behind something you love for something you *think* you are supposed to love. Lots of trends tend to follow the leader, but who actually is the leader and where are they going? Perhaps it wouldn't be so bad if Gray Crayon Syndrome was limited to coloring time or if the only people we were exposed to were those sitting at our table.

Today we are not only watching and observing our classmates and neighbors. Now we have billions of people on the Internet we can imitate! Look at any Pinterest board--the variety of ways we can spend our time, energy, and dollars could occupy a million lifetimes. Macramé, decorating with twine, pallet re-purposing, mason jar everything, pressed flowers, bird watching, photography, DIY teeth whitening, Ikea hacking, and so much more.

Facebook, Instagram, Snapchat, and Twitter all show us how we should look and how big the gap between our thighs should be. It is easy to get lost in the endless sea of choices. Who am I? What do I really love? How do I know if I genuinely love something, or if I love it because I think I am "s'posed to" love it?

[handwritten margin note: who is the real leader & where are they going?!]

28

Had I been an introspective five-year-old, I may have come up with an answer to these questions. Instead, it took me thirty more years to figure it out, and it all comes down to this single phrase:

"Does it spark joy?"

I love this concept, which is an idea I learned from reading an organizing book by Marie Kondo called **The Life-Changing Magic of Tidying Up**. She uses this phrase to help select which items should remain in your home or get tossed, but perhaps I should explain further how this helps in our day-to-day lives.

When I was thirty-three years old, I played my very first soccer game. A friend invited Jason and me to join a co-ed indoor soccer team. I was nervous, but I didn't let my anxiousness get in my way of trying something new. From the very first few minutes of the game, I was hooked. I loved it! I couldn't believe the rush I would get running up and down the field after that silly ball. I loved going shoulder to shoulder with an opponent against the wall. I couldn't believe how much exercise I could trick myself into doing.

As you can imagine, having never played soccer before, my footwork needed...work. But that didn't matter to me! I loved playing, and in time, I would go on to play many more seasons of co-ed and all-girls indoor soccer. Even when I shattered my wrist on my third game, I had the pros screw it back together--as soon as I was healed I was lacing up my cleats again. I love soccer; *it sparks joy*. I am not very good, yet, but soccer sparks joy!

Now, perhaps we can compare this to my apathy for softball. I grew up playing softball as a youth and many times as an adult on city leagues. I have played catcher, first baseman, and outfielder. I would say I am a *decent* player (insert false modesty here), and at times my batting was even considered phenomenal. But I just don't love it. I mean, softball is okay and I like doing it with my friends, but it just doesn't have the excitement and fun of soccer for me. I am better at softball than soccer, but it just doesn't spark joy. My friend Ashley, on the other hand, adores softball and plays any chance she can get. She lights up whenever she talks about it.

I hope you can tell which one of these activities sparks joy for me. If both events happened to be scheduled on a Thursday night, it would be pretty easy for me to pick which sport I would prefer to play. The trouble comes when I can play softball on Tuesday and soccer on Thursday. Do I still play softball, even though it's just okay?

What if we identified the activities in our lives that sparked joy for us, while eliminating the ones that were just okay? Imagine a life filled with things that spark joy for you! A coffee can full of purple crayons in various shades!

"When you recover or discover something that nourishes your soul and brings joy, care enough about yourself to make room for it in your life."
— Jean Shinoda Bolen (6)

What are the purple crayons in your life? I can help you identify them. Close your eyes. Wait, not yet! Read this first, then close your eyes and picture yourself enjoying your favorite activity. Maybe it's a sport, or perhaps something more leisurely. Are you thinking about a hobby, a special place, or being with a special person? I want you to really think about it. What does it look like when you are engaged in this thing or event; what are the sights, sounds, smells, and feelings you have? Is your heart racing or is it calm and relaxed? Picture everything about this activity.

Are you smiling, looking forward to when you can enjoy this activity again? Pay attention to how it makes you feel. Okay, close your eyes now. Do it! Closing your eyes helps your brain to picture it better.

Once you have found that image and felt the joy of doing the activity, try to hold onto it for just a minute. This feeling is your new ruler. This is how you can judge between the things you love and the things you think you're "s'posed to" love. This feeling of joy is a great way to measure new things that come into your life and an even better way to cut out some of the gray crayons in your world.

To do this, you must ask yourself, "Does this spark joy like soccer sparks joy?" Well, perhaps for you it wouldn't be soccer, so insert whatever it is that you pictured.

"Does this spark joy like _____ sparks joy?"

Now what if you closed your eyes...and you thought of nothing? I invite you to not freak out about that. Congratulations, if you thought of nothing, you are Julia Roberts!

Have you watched the movie Runaway Bride? (You should, it's darling.) Julia Roberts plays a bride in this movie and has a little habit of leaving her would-be grooms at the altar, making her the town joke. Enter Richard Gere, the big city reporter who is looking for a good story. As her next wedding day approaches, he interviews her family, friends, and several of her former fiancés. With each guy Richard Gere interviews, he asks them if they remember how she liked her eggs. Each one would answer, "Over easy, same as me," or "Sunny side up, just like I like them," each ex with a different answer.

I won't ruin the ending for you, but in the story Julia Roberts' character decides to figure out how she likes her eggs, independent of anyone else's opinion.

If you couldn't think of what sparks joy for you, congratulations Julia! It's time to start figuring out what does spark joy. Sunny side up or poached? The only way to do that is to get out there and start trying new things.

Truly, everything we needed to know we learned in kindergarten.

Use the things you know that "Spark Joy" in your life to evaluate other activities.

Cut out those things that don't measure up.

You can get in trouble for copying others--forget the masses (and social media!) and avoid the Gray Crayon Syndrome.

Create your own bold masterpiece with your purple crayon in hand.

In Other(s) Words

"Comparison is the thief of joy."
— Theodore Roosevelt

"The reward for conformity is that everyone likes you but yourself."
– Rita Mae Brown

"Remember always that you not only have the right to be an individual,
you have an obligation to be one."
– Eleanor Roosevelt

"Be yourself; everyone else is already taken."
— Unknown

"I think everybody's weird. We should all celebrate our individuality
and not be embarrassed or ashamed of it."
-- Johnny Depp

Helping Others

One of the best compliments I have ever received was from a friend who told me, "It must be fun to be you." This comment made me stop in my tracks and think about her words. It is fun to be me! And, it was so nice to have the reminder. When you recognize someone having real joy in an activity, point that out to them. It can look something like this: "Do you realize you light up when you talk about_____? You must have a lot of fun being you!"

Ed(you)cation

Write a list of twenty activities or things that "Spark Joy" in you. Choose one of these and write down what about this activity or thing sparks joy. For example: indoor soccer sparks joy because I get great exercise without even knowing it; I get an adrenaline rush when I go shoulder to shoulder down the wall for the ball; I get out aggression that builds up during the week; I like the feeling of trying harder each game.

Okay, your turn! List away!

1. Creating - quilting
2. Creating - scrapbooking
3. playing with my kids
4.
5.
6.
7.
8.
9.
10.
11.
12.
13.
14.
15.
16.
17.
18.
19.
20.

JOURNAL

"Through fear of knowing who we really are we sidestep our own destiny, which leaves us hungry in a famine of our own making...we end up living numb, passionless lives, disconnected from our soul's true purpose. But when you have the courage to shape your life from the essence of who you are, you ignite, becoming truly alive."

−Dawna Markova

TO KNOW ME IS TO LOVE ME

♡ *works on yourself too!*

One of my all-time favorite phrases is, "To know me is to love me." Although I have always loved this phrase, I didn't always realize that it was the key to self-confidence. So, how do you come to love yourself and know yourself? Let's look at some examples.

Consider the first time you had to put gas in your car on your own. Were you confident? The first few times I gassed up my car, I thought I was going to screw something up. There were so many buttons and steps, and I was sure I was going to blow up the gas station. I was not very confident, and I am sure I looked as nervous as I felt as I hesitantly did each step.

Today, however, I get fuel all the time (pretty much constantly, really). I don't even give it a second thought whenever I pull up to the pump. I know the steps, and I know the twenty questions the pump will ask me: is this credit or debit? Do you want a car wash? Do you want a receipt? Like us on Facebook. Burritos are 2/$1.00. (Just give me my gas already...it's freezing out here!) I know I'll have to select the grade, lift the nozzle, begin pumping, and wait for it to finish.

(Here is a tip: when you gas up your car and it isn't freezing outside, take a minute to remove any trash from your car. It's a great way to keep it tidy.)

random & awesome!

I digress! The point of all this is after years of fueling up again and again, I know how to do it confidently, and it doesn't cause me any anxiety. I am confident because I know my stuff.

We don't always know ourselves. Sure, some of us can tell you all about the latest trends in fitness, fashion, home décor, maybe even Pokemon Go, the products we sell at work, or the ins and outs of our hobbies, but we are not always as thorough with our knowledge about ourselves. We have degrees in topics ranging from communication to business, but we haven't mastered the art of "me."

I want you to get a Master's degree in you. I want to help you with your Ed(you)cation. You need to get to know you. Become the expert on You. To know yourself is to love yourself, and this self-love is self-confidence.

"You are you. Now, isn't that pleasant?"
— Dr. Seuss

Although there will be several tips throughout this book on how to get to know yourself, I would like to direct you to some specific things that can help you uncover the ins and outs and layers of you.

1. Personal Assessment Tests

I love personal assessment tests. I try to take as many assessments as I can because I learn something about myself every time. Do I think they are always accurate? No, but even in inaccuracy I learn about myself. I pay attention to how I respond to the results. What did I like about the results? What tickles me?

For example, I took a test and it told me I have WOO (Winning Others Over). I love that I have WOO! I do like to win others over, and I am happy this is one of my strengths. This is not implying I am a con artist; I want to win others over to a new way of thinking about themselves. I imagine WOO is dangerous in the hands of those who want to scam you--I am sure many a dictator has developed their WOO--thankfully, and fortunately for you, my heart is good.

In that same test, I learned that being strategic was my number one skill. This intimidated me, and I thought that perhaps I had cheated the test somehow, that I wasn't strategic enough to deserve it as my number one. I thought if someone found out that I had strategy among my strengths, they would compare it to their strategy, and they would think mine fell short. Then I calmed myself down and started to look for how my strategic strength showed up in my life. I can see it now, and can see how I can bless others with it.

I took another assessment once that talked about my energy, that I have the ability to do many projects at once, and that I actually finish those projects. I learned a lot about myself from this. The knowledge and awareness of this energy helped me embrace that side of me. I used to think that if you did too many projects at once, people would think you were flighty and not really accomplishing anything. On the contrary, this test helped me discover that although I do have a lot of projects going at one time, that energy and productivity feeds my soul. And I am a finisher!

I also learned that because I am running in so many direction at once, I should partner with someone who can be an anchor for me so I can finish the task at hand in a timely manner. One of my best anchors is my sister Kelsey--she is the calm to my frenzy.

Right, wrong, or "I can't see it yet," assessments help me learn things about myself.

Some of my favorite assessment tests are:

Ø StrengthsFinders through the Gallup Institute:
This test does have a cost, for $15.00 you can get a list of your top five strengths. If you want a more complete list, the purchase price is a bit more. I found having my top five to be really helpful. My top five are: Strategic, Learner, Input, Maximizer, and WOO (Winning Others Over) You can find the test at www.gallupstrengthscenter.com.

Ø Enneagram:
This personality assessment has nine types. Now part of me says "you don't know me!" and I wonder if you can fit the whole world's unique population into nine different types. However, I did gain insight

from this test about myself. I am in search of anything that can help me get a master's degree in me. From the Enneagram Institute, here are the nine different types: The Reformer, The Helper, The Achiever, The Individualist, The Investigator, The Loyalist, The Enthusiast, The Challenger, and The Peacemaker. I like that the Institute goes further to suggest how different types may interact with one another, as well as identifying downsides of these types and how to overcome them. www.enneagraminstitute.com

Ø **Five Love Languages:**

Learning how you like to receive love can also help you to recognize and express love to those in your circle in a language they can understand. My love language is Words of Affirmation. I love words. For Christmas, Mother's Day, birthdays, I just want a piece of paper with words on it about how you feel about me. I treasure any note my husband leaves me. Don't get me wrong, this girl loves a good gift, but it isn't my love language. The five different love languages are Words of Affirmation, Acts of Service, Receiving Gifts, Quality Time, and Physical Touch. www.5lovelanguages.com

Ø **Dressing Your Truth:**

This assessment helps you to dress on the outside true to your nature within. For example, if you wear soft demure colors with little flowers but then you come across as strong, organized, assertive, and powerful, the way you dress isn't being congruent with who you are. This discord between your appearance and your demeanor can put people off because they can sense that disconnect, leaving them unsure what to expect from you. Think of it like a package; if you opened a bag of chips expecting Doritos, but instead it contained salt and vinegar chips, your taste buds would be confused! This assessment also has some personality features to it that helped me understand my energy level and accept it just the way it is. Even if others have energy that is calm and still, my energy level has become a joy to me and is needed in the world.

The best part of Dressing Your Truth is you can dial into what colors, shapes, and textures look best for you. Who doesn't like a little help as they shop?? Those sneaky advertisers make everything look good. I am type 3 on this assessment. (7)

2. Asking Others *← a personal progress experience*

You can ask those in your circle to help you understand some of your best qualities. If you confide in people you look up to and respect, they can give you the best insight to yourself. Just because you may not recognize the same things they see within you, it doesn't mean those qualities aren't there. It simply means you need some time to ponder on it. Start looking for what they see in you. Ask them to write down these qualities so you can chew on it for a while, returning to it, and reviewing their list whenever you need.

3. Take Notice *pay attention be aware*

Get a small notebook to carry with you wherever you go. Give it a title, maybe something like, "Things About Me." Or maybe it just has your name, 'Kayla-Leah.' Write down anything and everything you discover about yourself over the next couple of weeks. Start paying attention to you with the intent of discovering things about yourself.

Be aware of the things you like and the things you dislike. Qualities in others you admire. Qualities in others you don't admire. All these things combined tell you a story about yourself.

Look for patterns in your behavior. Are you a night owl? Do you work best with deadlines? (Some people use the word procrastinator, but I prefer, "I work best with deadlines.") Do you get energized being around people or do you recharge best alone? In the morning, are you like cheese and get better with time or are you the early bird that sings to bring in the sun?

> *"Use the creative process--singing, writing, art, dance, whatever-- to get to know yourself better."*
> *-Catie Curtis*

Keep in mind: we are constantly growing and changing. We have so many seasons in our life! Just as trees change throughout the year, you could describe your leaves as green in the spring, but come fall that wouldn't be true. In fall they are yellow, or perhaps orange. The qualities you discover are not always absolutes. Perhaps if your list of dislikes included onions, at some point down the road you may discover

41

you have come to love them. You may be early riser now, but perhaps in a different season you may gravitate toward being a night owl.

You are the only one who gets to be the authority on you. You get to choose who speaks into your life.

When you are an authority on yourself you can also advocate for what you need. Recently I was in the mountains of Idaho and had the opportunity to zip-line. I was very intentional about asking the guides for what I needed and what to expect. Since I'm the authority on me, I knew I did not want to stand on the towering platform for ten minutes while harnesses were checked and waiting for the all clear. I knew that delay would allow too much time for doubt to build, and I might have backed out of the adventure. While we were on the ground, I spoke up and asked the guide to check all my gear before we went up so when I got on the platform I could just go. The experience was completely different because I confidently recognized, asked for, and received what I knew I needed to make zip-lining fun and successful for me. I got on the platform and just let go--and it felt glorious!

The more you know about yourself, the more confident you can become in you.

"It is the individual who knows how little they know about themselves who stands the most reasonable chance of finding out something about themselves before they die."
– S. I. Hayakawa

Your confidence and knowledge will enable you to advocate for what you need at work, in relationships, and in new situations. Take time to discover yourself through the lens of others through assessments, asking others, and taking notice. Be intentional about getting your Master's Degree of YOU!

In Other(s) Words

"To love oneself is the beginning of a life-long romance."
- Oscar Wilde

"You cannot be lonely if you like the person you're alone with."
-Wayne Dyer

Helping Others

Share, share, share! When you take a personality assessment, share it with others and encourage them take it as well. Help them to see their good qualities discovered through the assessments. Sometimes we just need a little help, and you can be that person for someone else. Be aware that they may have a different reaction than expected; be a coach and help them see that their uniqueness is a good thing.

Insight of God

There is much to be learned by the relationships and interactions of God with his prophets in the Bible. Abraham and Isaac stand out because of the extreme example of God asking Abraham to sacrifice his most beloved, long-awaited son, Isaac. Abraham was obedient and prepared to do as God had required. He made all the arrangements and even raised the knife to slay his son. Mercifully, God intervened and Abraham was praised for his willingness to be obedient in all things.

Did God need to know Abraham was willing to be obedient in all things? If one believes God is all-knowing, then one would believe God already knew Abraham. (We learn this in Jeremiah 1:5, "Before I formed thee in the belly I knew thee; and before thou camest forth out of the womb I sanctified thee.") God knew that Abraham would be obedient.

This leaves us something to ponder. Perhaps the whole event wasn't for God to learn something about Abraham. What if the point was that Abraham needed to learn something about Abraham?

God wanted Abraham to learn that Abraham is faithful, obedient, and God serving.

What does God want you to know about you? What situations has He allowed in your life so you can get your Master's Degree? God desires for us to know ourselves as He knows us. Take every opportunity available to get to know you, and your confidence will increase.

43

Ed(you)cation

Pick one assessment from above to discover more about you. Write your reactions here and list what you have discovered about yourself.

JOURNAL

"Because one believes in oneself, one doesn't try to convince others. Because one is content with oneself, one doesn't need others' approval. Because one accepts oneself, the whole world accepts him or her."
– Lao-Tzu

THE GREEN HUTCH PARABLE

One day a few years ago, I received a phone call from my brother, Tobias. He knows I always have my hands in a project or two and that I enjoy redoing furniture from time to time.

"Hey sis, I found this awesome desk thing at a garage sale. It's handmade, and I think you'll like it. Do you want it?"

I couldn't resist--later that day my brother dropped by my house and delivered a huge hutch. It was very...unique. I didn't quite love it, but the piece was very sturdy and solid and had several nooks and crannies desperate to hold something. Inspired by a bold candy apple green tote in my garage, I dashed to the store to buy some paint and other supplies. I began painting the piece immediately.

After I put one generous layer of paint on, I let it dry for several hours. I was then able to age it up a bit, scratching and removing the paint in certain areas to reveal the richly colored wood underneath. I had even put yellow paint as an under-layer in certain spots and intentionally sanded that area to allow a peek of yellow.

I'll confess, the outcome was luscious. I loved the amazing result, and I knew that I just had to keep the hutch. I decided it would be perfect for storing my fabric, notions, and threads, not to mention bringing even more color to my fiber art studio. I left the hutch in the garage to cure for a few days while I made room for this new treasure in my sewing studio.

My family is quite close, and although my mother knew my brother had bought me a piece of furniture from a yard sale, the hutch wasn't the reason she paid me a visit later that week. She had come to see the litter of farm kittens that had been born in our storage room within the garage. In my excitement over the kittens, I had forgotten all about the hutch when I eagerly took my mom out to see our new furry tribe.

As soon as we stepped into the garage, she took one look at the hutch and turned to me. "I am so glad you are re-doing that hutch," she said. "It is hideous! What an ugly color!"

I stared back at her and realized she was serious. I laughed right out loud. "Mom, this is the after. I already re-finished it."

Mortified, she quickly apologized, backpedaling as fast as she could. She would have never, ever said something like that to me had she known I had already painted it.

I tried to assure her again and again that my feelings were fine, finally expressing, "Mom, it's okay! I love it enough for both of us!"

And I truly did. I loved my green hutch so much it didn't matter to me that she didn't like it, even though she thought it was hideous. Because the hutch wasn't meant for her, it was meant for me.

All that mattered was I loved it. I was so in love with it that her disparaging words had delivered no sting. Let me say that again: her words had no sting because I loved it.

When we have things in our lives that we truly love, or when we truly love ourselves, it doesn't matter what anyone else thinks. We can have enough self-love for "both of us."

My mother would never have criticized the hutch had she known I had already toiled and labored to turn it into something I loved. But I am glad she did. Her reaction to the hutch helped me realize that if you

48

love something enough, that love has the power to take away any sting life can throw at you. That love dulls our need to look to others for approval, because we'll have enough approval and love for ourselves.

"Let yourself be drawn by the stronger pull of that which you truly love."
— Jalaluddin Rumi

This is what a confident life looks like.

We will encounter people along our way who don't like us, who don't love something we do, or don't respect who we are. Others might not love our sense of style, our hobbies, or our form of self-expression. In fact, they may make a special effort to be very vocal about their disapproval toward us. Unfortunately, this can't always be avoided.

"Whatever course you decide upon, there is always someone to tell you that you are wrong. There are always difficulties arising which tempt you to believe that your critics are right. To map out a course of action and follow it to an end requires courage."
– Ralph Waldo Emerson

The key to feeling self-confident among the voices of criticism at work, at school, or even at home is to really learn to love you enough for everyone.

"You yourself, as much as anybody in the entire universe, deserve your love and affection."
– Buddha

Getting to know yourself is one way to love yourself enough for everyone. Another key is to focus on filling your life with things that spark joy. Loving yourself enough for everyone is a process, but it is worth the journey.

In Other(s) Words

"It took me a long time not to judge myself through someone else's eyes."
– Sally Field

"Do your thing and don't care if they like it."
— Tina Fey, Bossypants

"Wouldn't it be powerful if you fell in love with yourself so deeply that you would do just about anything if you knew it would make you happy? This is precisely how much life loves you and wants you to nurture yourself. The deeper you love yourself, the more the universe will affirm your worth. Then you can enjoy a lifelong love affair that brings you the richest fulfillment from inside out."
-Alan Cohen

Insight of God

Throughout the New Testament and in Matthew chapter 19 Vs. 19, we are reminded of the commandment to "Love thy neighbor as thyself." This verse teaches we should love our neighbor and treat them according to the Golden Rule. For those struggling with self-love, however, this counsel needs to be reversed. We know how we should treat our neighbor yet we forget how to treat ourselves. In my opinion we are asked to do both, to love ourselves and love our neighbor. Joel Osteen says, "Don't ever criticize yourself. Don't go around all day long thinking, 'I'm unattractive, I'm slow, I'm not as smart as my brother.' God wasn't having a bad day when he made you... If you don't love yourself in the right way, you can't love your neighbor. You can't be as good as you are supposed to be."

Helping Others

If you enjoy a quality in someone, let them know! Help them recognize and find joy in those attributes you enjoy. Be specific in your praise. One way to do this is through asking questions, such as, "Do you realize you are really (insert positive quality here)?"

Ed(you)cation

List forty things you love about yourself. This may seem difficult at first--you might have to ponder and dig deep. This list may take some time. Don't skip. Don't skimp. Forty things! Examples from my list: I love my sense of humor, I love how I make friends with everyone, I love my spontaneity. Ready, Go!

1. _____
2. _____
3. _____
4. _____
5. _____
6. _____
7. _____
8. _____
9. _____
10. _____
11. _____
12. _____
13. _____
14. _____
15. _____
16. _____
17. _____
18. _____
19. _____
20. _____
21. _____
22. _____
23. _____
24. _____
25. _____
26. _____
27. _____
28. _____
29. _____
30. _____
31. _____
32. _____
33. _____
34. _____
35. _____
36. _____
37. _____
38. _____
39. _____
40. _____

JOURNAL

"Mark My Words, My Words In Other Words Are Not Just Words."
— Syed Sharukh

WORDS MATTER

I was bullied every day for a long time. My bully was constantly putting me down, telling me I was stupid, ugly, a slob, and not liked by anyone. The worst was when I was told I was an awful mom.

These cutting remarks were always spoken in whispers so no one else could hear or defend me. Whenever I had an accomplishment, my bully would downplay my role, or remind me of my other screw-ups. It got to the point where my bully was following me as I went around town, even coming to my home to bully me. I was conflicted because I felt like this person was a close friend, which is probably why I let this go on for years.

I am sure as a friend you would have counseled me to break up with this person, or maybe even encourage me to file a restraining order for the constant attacks.

But I couldn't, because this bully was myself. The negative self-talk and bullying was all in my own head, spoken in my own voice. Most people probably weren't aware of the constant, poisonous inner dialogue I was having. The negative thoughts in my head were not that severe, I reasoned, so I let it go on for much longer than I should have. I knew the negative self-talk was harmful, but I didn't know how much negative self-talk I had let seep into every aspect of my life.

Anytime I felt like I was doing well at something, a thought would cut through my mind trying to negate any positive feelings I might have enjoyed. If I made a good dinner for my family, I would recall all the other times I hadn't. Whenever I woke up early to exercise, I would discourage myself by thinking, "I probably won't keep this up." I would notice the good qualities I saw in others--they would seem so amazing compared to the shameful and imperfect image I had created of myself in my mind.

I finally got to the point where I was willing to break up with my bully. I learned how powerful words can be. Often, we say things to ourselves that we first, would never say to anyone else, and second, would never allow anyone else to say to us.

I encourage you to break up with your bully. Break the cycle of negative thoughts. I want to teach you how to issue a restraining order against your bully with guidelines of keeping your bully at bay. It can be so easy to get down and depressed with a constant barrage of criticism coming from within--it's time to stop!

Words matter, and the words we use about ourselves matter. Our words truly have the power to create or destroy our world, whether they are spoken or unspoken. Our thoughts and words we use about ourselves have an influence on us. If you are constantly telling yourself you are fat, saying things about your thunder thighs and cracking fat jokes, then chances are you will start to see yourself as fat and will treat yourself accordingly.

Your words can become a self-fulfilling prophesy. I once saw a meme that said, "I wish I was the size I was when I first thought I was fat." The idea was funny but also, sadly, a little true. Compare that to someone who tells themselves daily that they are an athlete. They have a different mindset on how they view their body and life. Their words affect the way they eat, think, and move in this world.

I tease my husband and tell him I talk to people about the voices in their heads. Really, what I do is try to help people to recognize this constant dialogue going on inside their minds that we need to address. What are the words that run through our mind throughout the day?

Are they words like I am kind, I am hard working, I am beautiful? Or do they sound a little more like this:

I am so forgetful.
I am always late.
I am fat.
I am so dumb.
I am ugly.
I will never be anything special.
I'm failing.
I am an awful mother.
He is so much better at this.
I am such a fake.
If they only knew the real me.

The reason our thoughts matter is because the words we think and say are commands for our body. I learned how to use a computer using a DOS prompt. To operate the computer, you had to type in every command: C:/run, C:/stop. You would insert one command at a time to get the computer to do what you wanted. (This pre-dated the beautiful graphics and operating systems on our current computers.) Our bodies and minds are designed to execute the commands we give them through thoughts and words in the same way the prompts told the computer what to do. The relationship between how we talk to ourselves and how we actually see ourselves is fascinating.

Being intentional about only giving your body good commands is important because it's a step toward becoming your best, most confident self.

When we give ourselves commands, we need to frame everything in the positive. I wouldn't type in C:/don't stop into the computer, I would type in C:/run. Instead of telling yourself, "I am not fat", instead say I am healthy and strong". Tell yourself, "I am mindful" instead of "I don't forget things".

Ideally, we would only speak and think positive thoughts about ourselves. However, as you work on this new habit of positive self-talk, you may find yourself letting a negative statement creep in. Don't get down on yourself--you can always correct this! When I am trying to talk more patiently and kindly to my children and I forget and start to talk in a tone I don't like, I stop and try to change it by the end.

"I asked you to take out the trash!" (At this point I realize I am grumpy and want to change.) "You silly kiddo, thanks for doing it for me."

The same thing can apply with our self-language. As we recognize negative statements from our mind or our mouth, we have the power to change them. You don't have to be held captive by this old, unhealthy habit.

For a time, I had to focus on teaching my son a better way to talk to me and others. I would pretend I was holding a remote in my hand that controlled him. I would say, "Stop!" while holding my imaginary remote and pushing a button. "Let's try that again, but a little nicer." I would then say, "Rewind!" He would even have fun with it and walk backwards when I hit rewind. I would say, "Play!" and push another imaginary button, giving him chance at a do-over.

Cute idea

We can all make space for do-overs or replays. We can weed out our old, bad habits and replace them with new, positive ones.

How is this done? Recognition is the first step:

1. Name bully thoughts for what they are:

"That is a negative thought," or "That was negative. I want to use positive language."

2. You can re-phrase what you just said in positive, constructive terms.

I was recently volunteering at my son's school and passed a bulletin board with these wonderful do-over examples on it:

Instead of Saying:	Try Saying:
This is too hard......	What am I missing?
I made a mistake.	Mistakes help me improve.
I don't understand.	I am on the right track.

I'll never be as smart as her.	I am going to figure out what she is doing.
I will never get it.	I will use some of the strategies I have learned.
I can't get this.	This may take some time and effort.
I give up.	I am going to keep trying.

3. You could even mix both, naming, and reframing words.

"I am always late!" Wait, that was negative. "I am mindful about being on time." The technique may sound simple and perhaps a little silly, but the application does really have a way of disrupting old patterns.

Being nice to yourself with words matters. As you develop confidence about yourself, your language will change and as your language changes, you will feel even more confident.

A few years ago, as I was tucking my youngest son into bed, on a whim I told him, "You are smart, special, and important to me. And I love you." Yes, these sentiments were a slight knock off from The Help. I didn't care, because it felt so good saying those things to him. A good mommy moment for sure.

The next evening when I tucked him in he asked me in the sweetest voice, "Could you say those things again?" Of course, I was delighted to! This went on for a few nights without any changes, but one night I began, "Porter, you are smart, special, important to me..."

"And generous," Porter added, raising a finger in the air.

"Oh, okay, and generous. And I love you."

I giggled to myself as I left the room, tickled that he piped up and added something to our list. It had never occurred to me that Porter was generous. At the time, I didn't even know if he knew what generous meant, but I love that he claimed being generous for himself. By claiming he was generous, I knew he would look for more opportunities to be generous. I would also look for evidence of his generosity

59

to reinforce and point out throughout the day. My eyes were opened.

Fast forward to today. We have added many things to this list; some things he added, some came from me, some were qualities his dad asked me to add, and others I felt impressed by God to add. Our list takes on a new order and rhythm as it gets longer. Here is his current list as part of our nightly routine:

"Porter, you are smart, special, important to me, creative, talented, artistic, hard working. You have an attitude of gratitude, you are a leader, a covenant keeper, a bucket filler. You are generous and kind, humorous, handsome, brave, insightful, a good reader, a master builder, obedient, an athlete. I love you, and you're awesome."

I love that he gets to hear these things every night and think about who he is and the qualities he has as he is going to sleep. I love that he and I both look for examples of the qualities on his list throughout the day. Think about what this can do for him as he develops character and discovers who he is in life. Think of how these words can and have built his confidence.

What if you went to bed every night and someone said a long list of all your qualities to remind you of who you are? How would it change how you walked in your life?

In Other(s) Words

"Plant a thought and reap a word;
plant a word and reap an action;
plant an action and reap a habit;
plant a habit and reap a character;
plant a character and reap a destiny."
-Bishop Beckwaith

"Once you replace negative thoughts with positive ones, you'll start having positive results."
-Willie Nelson

"Talk to yourself like you would to someone you love."
-Brene Brown

60

"Much more surprising things can happen to anyone who, when a disagreeable or discouraged thought comes into his mind, just has the sense to remember in time and push it out by putting in an agreeable, determinedly courageous one. Two things cannot be in one place."
— Frances Hodgson Burnett, The Secret Garden

"You have been criticizing yourself for years, and it hasn't worked. Try approving of yourself and see what happens."
— Louise L. Hay

"Every time words are spoken, something is created. Be conscious of what you say and how you say it. Use words that build up, appreciate, encourage and inspire."
-Lucy MacDonald

Insight of God

I believe there is a divine pattern sent to us in the Bible that encourages us to claim I AM statements.

In Exodus 3:14 it says, "And God said unto Moses, I AM THAT I AM."

God declared, "I Am, That I Am."

Throughout the Bible we are told that we are the children of God. As His children, we have inherited the traits of God, much like we inherit the traits of our earthly parents: brown eyes, red hair, extroverted personality, etc.

I believe that God wants us to recognize these traits and nourish them within ourselves. Just like my son claimed generous as one of his traits, you need to claim the I AM statements in your life.

We can claim the Godly things in us!
I am patient.
I am kind.
I am loving.
I am honest.

These I AM statements are like seeds. If I plant seeds in the ground and then put a stick with a picture of a cantaloupe at the end of the row, I know that is where I planted cantaloupes. When you come to my garden and we look at the dirt, I say, "These are my carrots, these are my peppers, these are my cantaloupes." You don't protest and say, "That's not cantaloupe, that is dirt!" You believe me that cantaloupe will one day grow there.

When my garden grows with nourishment and care, I would show you the little green stems poking through the earth with bright little leaves. You would not claim, "That is not cantaloupe!" because I have told you that is where I am growing my cantaloupe. When the first blossoms appear, or the first small round melons arrive, you still do not deny that this is cantaloupe. Finally, the day comes when we harvest the fruit, slice it open, and enjoy the sweetness together.

The same is true with our words. By saying, "I am…" you are putting a stick at the end of the row in your garden with the name of your plant on it. You don't have to have the fruit before you claim it.

I am hoping this analogy will give you permission to make I AM statements, no matter in what stage of growth or harvest you find yourself. However, the garden analogy isn't entirely accurate, because you don't have to plant anything to reap the fruit.

God has already planted seeds of divinity within us. I am going to tell you this again, so pay attention: WE DON'T HAVE TO PLANT ANYTHING. GOD HAS ALREADY PLANTED SEEDS OF DIVINITY WITHIN US! All we need to do is mark the row with "I am…" (I am patient, I am generous, I am kind), nourishing the mound of dirt and watching for evidence of growth. The more we nourish and care, the more growth we will see. As we see the evidence of growth, it becomes easier to believe what we have hoped for within ourselves is true. The best part of all comes when we finally get to enjoy the harvest.

You can begin with claiming the things you are or that you want to become with I AM statements.

Here is a word of caution: be careful what you grow. Speaking and thinking any words is a type of nourishing, and nourishing weeds creates growth, too. If we are not cautious we can grow doubt, fear, insecurity, and unworthiness, and these can choke out good seeds if we allow them to take over.

In Matthew 7:20 it reads, "Wherefore by their fruits ye shall know them."

I hope we can choose to nourish the seeds of divinity within us by posting a sign at the end of the row that says "I am...." As you see evidence of this divinity, I hope you can look forward to the fruits.

Helping Others

Help others see the power of their words by naming and reframing their negative statements for them. I often tell people, "Be nice to you, that was a very negative thing to say." I then rephrase it for them so they can see a model of positive language. Can I give you permission to borrow phrases from The Help also? "You is smart, you is kind, you is important." Or borrow mine: "You are smart, special, important to me. And I love you." Share these with those you love. Show them the power of words.

Ed(you)cation

1.   Wear a rubber-band on your wrist for one week. Pay attention to your thoughts and words. Whenever you say something unkind about or to yourself, snap the rubber band. This will help you associate the sting that comes with each of those negative thoughts and words. This will make you aware of just how often we say negative things to ourselves.

2.   Write a list of forty I AM statements. It is okay if these are seeds, not full-grown plants or fruit. If it helps, you can pick a quality you admire and write it as an I AM statement for yourself. If you want to have the harvest, then write it in an I AM statement.

For my list I would write:
I am patient.
I am generous.
I am kind.
I am a good mother.
I am a rock star wife.
I am a good friend.
I am charitable.
I am confident.

Now come up with 40 of your own:
1. _____
2. _____
3. _____
4. _____
5. _____
6. _____
7. _____
8. _____
9. _____
10. _____
11. _____
12. _____
13. _____
14. _____
15. _____
16. _____
17. _____
18. _____
19. _____
20. _____
21. _____
22. _____
23. _____
24. _____
25. _____
26. _____
27. _____
28. _____

29. _____

30. _____

31. _____

32. _____

33. _____

34. _____

35. _____

36. _____

37. _____

38. _____

39. _____

40. _____

JOURNAL

"You have to love yourself or you'll never be able to accept compliments from anyone."
--Dean Wareham

ACCEPTING COMPLIMENTS

When someone pays you a compliment, what is your natural reaction? Do you thank them for their kind words, or do you diminish their gesture, excusing away their uplifting remarks or putting yourself down in response?

"Your song was so beautiful!"
"Thanks, but I didn't hit the high note at the end. I thought it sounded horrible."

"Your hair is so cute."
"Ugh, it is awful. It won't lay flat in the back."

"Your speech was amazing!"
"Really? You don't think it was a little slow at the beginning?"

Learning to accept a compliment without using self-deprecating language in return is part of developing your confidence. Nothing oozes insecurity like not being able to receive a compliment graciously.

Some people really struggle with knowing what to say after being praised. Maybe they don't agree with the accolades, or perhaps they do, but don't want to appear boastful. I have come across a few phrases you can keep handy to help you respond to compliments using confident language.

1. "Thank you."

Keep it simple! Our goal is to say thank you without caveats, excuses, or denial. This can be tough if everything inside us wants to add something negative. "Thank you" can be the goal, but if you are not there yet, you can try the second suggestion

2. "Thank you," plus...

"Thank you for taking the time to say so."
"Thank you; I was hoping it would go well."

Add something to your expression of gratitude for the compliment if it makes you feel more comfortable. Keep it brief and concise, and nothing derogatory. This recognizes the person giving the compliment without taking away value of what they said, or value from yourself. The "thank you," plus... does not come across as boastful and can ease you into being more comfortable with receiving praise.

3. Use Humor

"You say all the right things!"
"Will you follow me around all day?"
"...go on..."
"Tell me more."
"You're my new best friend!"
"I KNOW! Right?!"
"Hey, it takes one to know one!"

Humor makes responding to compliments fun! Add a wink at the end and enjoy a good giggle together. This playful response recognizes that the other person has just identified something great in you and that their words made you feel good.

4. Sharing Credit

"Thank you, I really appreciated all the work Becky did to help me polish my performance."

"Thank you, I felt more confident because of your help."

"Thank you, I will share this compliment to our team who all contributed in this effort."

5. Save it for Later

"Thank you, I am going to put that in my pocket and save it for a rainy day."

This isn't just a cute saying, if you actually tuck the compliment away in your memory so you can pull it out later and take a look at it. Perhaps this person saw something in you that you haven't observed before. By pulling it out of your pocket, you can try to begin to see this in yourself.

It is helpful to be prepared to receive compliments. Confident people accept compliments graciously. Choose a few phrases to have handy when compliments come your way.

<u>In Other(s) Words</u>

"I can live for two months on a good compliment."
-- Mark Twain

"I have been complimented many times and they always embarrass me; I always feel they have not said enough."
-- Mark Twain

"I was very pleased with your kind letter. Until now I never dreamed of being something like a hero. But since you've given me the nomination I feel that I am one."
— Albert Einstein

"Everybody likes compliment."
— Abraham Lincoln

<u>Insight of God</u>

I experienced a period in my life where I didn't feel like a very good mother. I felt as though everybody else knew how to do this mothering thing, and I was just mucking up. On a particularly tough day, I received a card from an acquaintance. I opened the card and it said:

Kayla,

I just wanted to tell you how impressed I am as I watch you with your children. You are such a great example of patience and teaching. Thank you for showing me what great mothering looks like in action and giving me something to strive for.

Your Friend, Jennifer

I read that card and the last thing I thought of was, "Thank you!"

The card made me burst into tears. It really did.

These were the first thoughts that ran through my mind:

She thinks I am such an awful mother, and she is just trying to encourage me. (Try reading that line with a really whiney voice--that's the way it sounded in my head that day.)

A few minutes later, I thought:

Maybe she saw me do something right, but if she knew how I really mothered she wouldn't think the same thing. (Still very whiney, overwhelmed, and down on myself.)

I put her thoughts in my pocket and chewed on them for the rest of the day. This is the conclusion I finally came up with:

Jennifer is an extremely busy and practically single mother, and she's in the master's program for counseling. She does not have time to blow air up my skirt. She does not have time to write nice, "encouraging" cards to just anyone. The timing is too perfect to not be divinely inspired. I know Jennifer to be a Godly woman and in touch with Him.

I realized that if Jennifer took time to send me this card, it wasn't because I needed to know that Jennifer thought I was a good mom. The reason she sent the card was because God wanted me to know that He feels I am a good mom.

Instead of casting this compliment away, I was able to think on it and see if it could be part of my truth. I have kept this letter to remind me of the many lessons I learned that day. Among them, I learned:

★ *1. I am a good mother.*
★ *2. Sometimes He sends messengers to deliver His messages of hope.*
★ *3. I want to be prepared to be His messenger for someone else.*
☆ *4. Don't cast out the good others see in you just because you don't see it within yourself yet.*

Helping Others

Compliment others! Be conscious about giving compliments. If those you compliment respond in a disparaging way, kindly and gently teach them a response they could give that honors your compliment and them.

Ed(you)cation

Pay attention to the compliments you hear others receive and how they respond to them. I learn how to respond to a compliment graciously even when I see others model it. I also learn how to not respond to a compliment when others disparage themselves. Watch, listen, learn, practice.

Respond to a compliment using the suggestions above, or come up with one of your own. Commit this day to always accept compliments graciously.

JOURNAL

"Life can only be understood backwards; but it must be lived forwards."
— Soren Kierkegaard

TIME TRAVELER

We watched a lot of "Back to the Future" when I was a kid. If you haven't seen the movies with Michael J. Fox, you still may be able to relate. There are several story plots in many movies and books that involve time machines or time travel. They usually all carry the same warning: do not change or interfere with anything from the past, or the consequences could be catastrophic. In the words of Doc from Back to the Future, it could cause "a chain reaction that would unravel the very fabric of the space-time continuum and destroy the entire universe!"

But even with these warnings, I often thought about time travel when I was younger. What if I could go back in time and change one or two things and have amazing outcomes. I could have taken first instead of second place in the state debate championships. I would have taken the corner slower and not rolled my car. I would have communicated with my boss better and not lost my high school job. In retrospect, these outcomes were all small potatoes.

As an adult, I have thought, what if I could go back in time and change some of our financial investments? Particularly the ones that ended up being fraudulent or resulted in complete loss of funds. Maybe I wouldn't have built that last house before the building bubble popped. Or finances aside, I would go back and I would keep my comments to myself instead of sharing some intense, judgmental feelings about another's choices. I would go back and put on sunscreen every day! ✼

Going back in time and changing the outcomes of our past is a fascinating idea, but if we could go back and alter things, would we really choose to do it? I don't know if we'll ever face that choice in reality--I have serious doubts that time travel will ever be a possibility. However, perhaps we can learn something from considering the hypothetical question: would I change the past?

The risks would possibly be too great--and I am not talking about the fabric of the space-time continuum-- but the risk that we would not be the same today if we had the ability to change yesterday. Would you risk changing a few things if it meant that you were not the same, if it altered your family or made your relationships different? Could modifying something in the past change everything that makes me, me? If it changed the people I have in my life today?

It might be incredibly tempting, if given the opportunity, to go back in time and change the negative aspects of our past. But what if we viewed our lives and our pasts, not as stand-alone events, but as a series of experiences designed to help us become the best version of ourselves?

With this new perspective, perhaps our desire to change the past would be decreased. I can tell you I have learned something valuable from each of the experiences I listed above. I can tell you that I like me, and I wouldn't risk losing all the wisdom I have learned from the past--the good, the bad, and the ugly.

Maybe this sounds all well and good for most of us, but what if your past includes trauma, abuse, or neglect? We are on this earth with other humans who sometimes make horrific choices. These choices can have such a huge impact on who we are that they stay with us for our entire lives. Perhaps this is where the "nevertheless" thought can come into play. Using "nevertheless" is a way to move forward, despite the trials of the past.

It looks a little something like this:
"I was neglected as a child, nevertheless, I grew to be mindful of others."
"I was abused by someone I trusted, nevertheless, I survived."

"I was the child of an addict, nevertheless, I am clean and I am a chain breaker."

These nevertheless statements take something negative from our pasts and permit us to find the "in spite of" result. Nevertheless allows us to accept the past and the fact that the past cannot be changed, while choosing to live in the here and now.

Our nevertheless statements don't correct or excuse the past hurts or diminish the past's wrongness. The "ends" of our survival and ability to thrive do not justify the "means".

I want to repeat: our survival and ability to thrive does not somehow justify or make right what happened to us.

Instead, we give ourselves permission to release the feelings of being blocked or stuck due to past circumstances we are helpless to change.

We do sometimes get stuck in the past, restricting ourselves from not able to truly live in the here and now. In the movie "Back to the Future", Marty McFly needed help to get back to his present, his help came in the form of a scientist and a bolt of lightning. Our "bolt of lightning", the ability to transport us to the here and now, can come in many forms. But I believe it is a choice. A choice to believe that we have the power to take any experience and use it for our good and make us stronger: we can stop the cycles of abuse, we can become better in spite of what has happened to us, or despite the choices we have made. We can live a nevertheless mindset.

Sometimes our "stuckness" in the past is pretty severe. Sometimes we need help building our time machine so we can have a bright future. For those who have suffered severe trauma, I suggest getting with a counselor, someone who has all the necessary tools at their disposal to help you rebuild. (A note here: finding the right counselor is like shopping for good shoes. It may take a bit of work and time to find the right size, style, and fit for you. Even once you find the right one, there is a breaking-in period. But once you find the right fit, you can really go places and make progress. Don't give up on counseling just because you haven't found the right fit yet.)

79

Another time travel issue we sometimes have is looking at the past and judging it by today's standards. We criticize our past choices and judge them by the knowledge and experience we have today. This pitfall only leads to misery. If I judge some of my past choices based on my current standards and knowledge, and then beat myself up over my mistakes, I am being unfair and cruel to myself.

The wisdom and experience that comes through life and living wasn't available to me back then. You can't take your height marked on the wall as a teen and compare it to your height now claiming that you fell short before. You hadn't yet had the time to grow! You were not the same person then as you are today. Yesterday you were different than you are today.

All our choices give us experience. When we know better, we do better. Quit judging your past choices on today's wisdom. Instead, be gentle with you. Be grateful for the experiences that taught you the wisdom you have today, even if it you earned it through trial and error. Even if it came through repeating an error again and again until we could narrow the gap between what we believe to be true and our ability to live it.

I have decided that if I could truly time travel, I would go back in time and give the younger Kayla a bit of encouragement. I would say, "Hang in there! You are going to make it! You will come through this trial brilliantly and stronger for it. It may be tough now, but nevertheless, you will come out amazing."

But I wouldn't change the past, because I would cease to be me.

About the Future.

Some familiar story lines that appear in second installment of Back to the Future happens when a character takes knowledge of the future and shares it with his past self. In this case, Biff took the winning horse races and sporting events found in a sports almanac and gave it to his younger self. The results made future Biff incredibly wealthy in the future. What if we could do the same but without any ethical consequences? What if we got an image of our future self and reverse-engineered it to see what choices we need to make today to make that future a reality?

And what if I told you this was truly possible?? No, it doesn't come in the form of a sports almanac, but rather in the form of dreams or wishes.

> *"The best way to predict the future is to create it."*
> *- Peter Drucker*

Let's say your "future you" is an author. What does present-day you need to do to become an author in the future?

We live in an amazing age. At our fingertips is much of the world's knowledge and wisdom on almost any subject. Never has there been so much information so easily accessible to the masses. Whatever your goals or dream, you can find information about it right this moment with a few key strokes and the help of your favorite search engine (thank you, Google).

Do you want to know how to harvest your own cotton to make into cloth? Google it. What about becoming a proficient at computers? Google. Play the ukulele? Google. Learn to sew, cook, clean, dance, yodel…or whatever to your heart's content. Knowledge is power. You can do something today to move you closer towards your goal.

So, you want to be an author? Start a blog today or join an online writing prompt group. Start an online writing group with your Facebook friends. Voraciously read good literature. Read about how others became authors. Research publishing options through Amazon and CreateSpace. Today you can do one thing to help you become an author tomorrow.

Just as words have power, so do images. A really powerful tool to create the future you want is in the form of a vision board. A vision board is a collection of images that represents the future you want. A vision board could be as simple as a poster filled with a collage of pictures: your dream vacation, a photo of a college graduate, an image related to your dream job.

The power behind a vision board is to pick visuals that create an emotion. For example, on one vision board I created I picked a picture of a swimming pool full of money. I didn't really want to fill a pool with money, but I did want to feel the abundance of being surrounded by money, floating in money, refreshed by money. Then I included pictures of college diplomas that I hoped to fund with that money, my dream car, images of service I could do with the funds that could fill a swimming pool.

Creating a vision board is one great way to help you get closer to your future dreams and goals.

You must, however, look at your vision board frequently to really give it the power it needs to drive you towards those goals.

You do have the choice to be a time traveler! You can review the past with a gentler lens and with the empowering word *nevertheless*. You can look to the future and rewind back to what you need to do today to achieve your desires. The way we view the past and the future affects our confidence.

<u>In Other(s) Words</u>

"The most beautiful people we have known are those who have known defeat, known suffering, known struggle, known loss, and have found their way out of the depths. These persons have an appreciation, a sensitivity and an understanding of life that fills them with compassions, gentleness, and a deep loving concern.
Beautiful people do not just happen."
– Elizabeth Kubler-Ross

"Happy people know they can either learn from the past or live in it."
--John Bytheway

"Forgiving does not erase the bitter past. A healed memory is not a deleted memory. Instead, forgiving what we cannot forget creates a new way to remember.
We change the memory of our past
into a hope for our future."
- Lewis B. Smedes

"Never be afraid to trust an unknown future to a known God."
— Corrie ten Boom

"People are like stained-glass windows. They sparkle and shine when
the sun is out, but when the darkness sets in their true beauty is
revealed only if there is light from within."
-Elisabeth Kubler-Ross

"Education is the passport to the future, for tomorrow belongs to
those who prepare for it today."
--Malcolm X

"The best way to predict the future is to create it."
-Peter Drucker

Insight of God

In the Old Testament in the book Genesis, Lot's family was told
to flee their home city. God was going to destroy the cities of Sodom
and Gomorrah. He commanded Lot and his family to "look not
behind thee" as they left. For those who are familiar with the story, we
know that Lot's wife looked back. In that moment, she was turned into
a pillar of salt.

In Luke Chapter 17 in the New Testament, Jesus counseled his
apostles on the importance of faith to encourage his disciples, and us,
to "Remember Lot's Wife". I believe it was a warning that faith is
forward looking. If we focus too much on looking back on the past,
we will miss what is right in front of us. What is in front of us is the
future filled with possibilities if we will only keep our eyes forward.
Remember Lot's wife. Don't look back.

Helping Others

People will often share their past experiences with us. Whenever
someone shares a story from their past with you, they are usually
seeking validation for the feelings they had from that experience.

83

Asking questions like, "How did that make you feel?" will give them an opportunity to focus on their feelings.

Mirror those feeling back to them. "So, that made you feel foolish," or "That made you angry because you were scared."

If your mirroring is correct, then move to validate those feelings. "I can see why you would be scared." Validation is powerful, and you can also take it one step further by helping with their nevertheless sentences or by helping them be kind to themselves in assessing the situation. Remind them they didn't know then what they know now.

Finally, telling them, "I wish I could go back to that moment and tell you everything was going to be okay," or "I wish I could have been there to help you," can be helpful. Asking, "What did you learn from this?" will help them to remember life experiences teach us just what we need to know.

Ed(you)cation

This Ed(you)cation may take a little extra time and effort. You may need to recruit the help a friend with the right kinds tools to work with you, such as a counselor, a life coach, or ecclesiastical leader. Seek this kind of help especially if your past has abuse or neglect. Refer to earlier sections in the chapter if necessary. Consider the following questions and journal.

List out some of your life's choices that have had some long-term consequences:

_____

_____

_____

List what you have learned from those experiences:

_____

_____

_____

List your nevertheless statements for these experiences:

_____

_____

_____

What advice would you give your younger self of the past?

_____

_____

_____

What is your plan to get unstuck from the past? A journal? Coach? Counselor?

_____

_____

_____

The future: Who is the future you going to be?

_____

_____

_____

What are some things you can do today to take a step toward that future you?

_____

_____

_____

What things might need to change in your life to make this future happen?

_____

_____

_____

JOURNAL

Shame is a soul eating emotion.
— C.G. Jung

SLAYIN' SHAME

Things fester when left hidden in the dark. I learned this the hard way while facilitating at a large women's conference. There were many moving parts I was involved with: a booth for my non-profit, hosting a workshop, speaking on the main stage, and helping behind the scenes with decorations, speakers, and other small details. My household suffered from what I called "Conference Neglect."

I came home one evening from the conference wanting to greet my family. I went to the room where my four boys like to congregate, and I opened the door. Whooooof! I was greeted with a putrid smell. It smelled like sweat and socks, briefs and teenage boy, all mixed in with something very rank and rancid. Now, my boys know they are not allowed to have food in their rooms, so of course the pungent smell had to have been caused by something else. Right?

Nope, the source of the agonizing odor was two plates of an unknown former food item that had been stashed under the bed for some indeterminate amount of time, definitely pre-conference.

"We need to air this place out!" I called them to action, although inside I was wanting to flip out and call in disaster control.

Things fester when left hidden in the dark, and the same is true for your most favorite thing you like to hide. Not chocolate--that actually has a pretty decent shelf life for hiding. No, I am talking about shame. I can't talk about confidence without likewise addressing your feelings of shame.

We tuck feelings of shame away, and why? Perhaps to address the shame another day? Maybe we hope the shame will disappear? We think there is nothing good that could come from bringing our shame to light.

What is shame exactly? Shame is not a feeling of "I did something wrong." That is something you do. Shame is a feeling of "I'm wrong," something we think we are.

I'm not good enough.
I am inadequate.
I am broken.
I am bad.
I am defective.
I am not worthy.

We hide these feelings under the proverbial bed or in the metaphorical closet. We don't want anyone to see them or know they exist. But despite our best efforts, the feelings of shame refuse to stay hidden under the bed. We haul our shame with us to work or out into the world like we were carrying it in a backpack. Shame comes along to affect our work, our relationships, the way we see ourselves, the way we see others, and the way we view our place in this world. We think we have hidden it, but our shame taints everything we do.

I have made it my mission to be the Shame Slayer. Women, especially, tend to carry a lot of shame. I have learned this first-hand through working with a program called Days For Girls. Many of us ladies are ashamed of our uteruses! This planet was peopled by periods, and we find shame in our menstruation for some reason. To me, this a little redonkulous, but it doesn't end there. We feel shame in our role as mothers, and we feel shame in how well we change between our different roles. WE compare ourselves to others, and we feel the shame when we don't feel like we measure up.

Being the Shame Slayer, I have discovered the way to slay shame is through VULNERABILITY.

Ooooh, did I lose you there? Yes, I said vulnerability. Who in their right mind wants to be vulnerable? I am pretty sure it makes the list of top ten things we humans would prefer to avoid. But if we want growth, we need to be vulnerable with each other and ourselves.

Vulnerability doesn't feel good; it feels like pulling back the rug and shouting, "Hey world, look what I have underneath here! Come judge me!"

You may be thinking, "My shame is fine just where it is, thank you very much." Is the effort it takes to expose and remove our shame worth the cost if vulnerability is the price we have to pay?

What's so bad about shame anyway?

Shame causes us to shrink. We get smaller, and we pull back from people, relationships, and situations. We shrink in fear that we will be discovered. Shame keeps us from connecting with people. Shame is the the barrier, the rock, that we set between us and others and it isn't helping us. Shame keeps us from living with confidence.

We feel disconnected even when we see other people doing things we would find shameful. We distance ourselves from that person or situation, not wanting anything to do with it. That distance keeps us from connecting with others.

What if I told you that I sucked my thumb until I was sixteen years old? Every day. Every spare moment. I sucked my thumb with a piece of cotton in my fingers.

What was your first reaction to this? You might be thinking, "That girl has some real issues; she's a mess; eeeew; wow, that's weird."
I hid my thumb-sucking from strangers, friends, and I even tried eventually to hide it from my family.

Maybe now you know this fact about me, you don't really want to be associated with me, Kayla-Leah #thumb-sucker.

I am going to be vulnerable and tell you what I believe is the reason I sucked my thumb for so long.

My mother struggles with mental illness. It isn't a condition she has asked for, and it's one she would willingly give up. She has struggled for many years to find help. She has been a constant guinea pig trying to find the right medication. She has endured many wrong medications including ones that made her break out in hives from head to toe, and one medicine caused her such excruciating physical pain all over her body, she didn't think she would make it through.

But the hives and the pain were not as bad as medicines that plain didn't work to help with the ache of depression.

When I was a child, there wasn't much information available on what was happening with my mother and how she could get help. Her coping mechanism when I was little was to stay in her bedroom in bed all day. She would do crossword puzzles, watch television, or crochet.

In the meantime, the six of us kids would run amuck. I would often sneak into my mom's room and ever so quietly sit on the edge of the bed. She had a waterbed so I would have to sit on the railing to not make any waves. If I made waves or if my energy was too much for my mom, she would send me out.

Mom was trying to cope the best she could with what she had available. I would never want to toss her under the bus because her struggle is so real, and she has spent a lifetime trying to find a way to endure, but as a young girl I didn't understand. I just knew I wanted my mom. I think my thumb-sucking, which was once an infantile behavior, became my comfort and my security, a way to self-soothe. It was my coping mechanism. *mine is to tune out...*

I am sure at some point it went from self-soothing to habit. I stopped sucking my thumb when I was sixteen years old because I wanted to kiss a boy. In my head, I couldn't picture being kissed by a boy and still being a thumb-sucker. So, I stopped. If only I had wanted to kiss a boy at a younger age!

92

When I told a crowd of nearly five-hundred women this story at a conference, I hadn't spoken about my thumb-sucking for nearly two decades. At first I felt them distance themselves (or maybe I was the one who created the distance with the fear of what they thought of me). However, when I shared my why in a very vulnerable way, I felt the distance shorten and I felt connection, love, and acceptance. I even had three women come up after and confide the age they stopped sucking their thumb, one woman well into her forties. My vulnerability helped her process some of her own shame.

I have hidden the shame of my thumb-sucking for my whole life. But the things we hide actually grow and fester--we need to air it out!

Think for a moment; what is your "thumb-sucking?" What is your shame? We will call it your X.

What happens when we hide something about ourselves? Either something we do, something we are, something that has happened to us? We go out and meet new people, and each new person knows nothing about X.

Perhaps they like us or respect us or want to kiss us! What happens to us mentally when we realize, "Oh, no. They don't know X about me. They don't know that habit, that shameful secret. They don't know what is under my rug. If they knew X, they wouldn't respect me, they wouldn't want to be associated with me, and they wouldn't want to be in my inner circle." We start feeling like there is a disconnect between who we are as we meet and interact with others, and who we really are with X. If we don't feel congruent between these two disconnected parts of ourselves, then it is difficult to walk with confidence.

I am asking you to pull back that rug and be vulnerable. In select situations, at least. You don't have to tell your boss you sucked your thumb for sixteen years, but could you tell your X to a friend, a counselor, a coach, an ecclesiastical leader? If you are vulnerable and share your X, then you can process through it. You can connect with yourself and others and feel that even with X you are worthy, you are accepted, and even loved

The Internet is full of stories of people being vulnerable. Loss of children, thoughts of suicide, struggling with a loved one's addictions. When you hear their vulnerable stories, you feel closer to them, even though most are complete strangers. You don't have to share your story in every setting with every audience. But there is power in vulnerability because it draws us closer. In the right setting at the right time, vulnerability becomes a power to connect, and to feel acceptance and love.

Sometimes we feel like we are fake or frauds, because we act one way in public while dealing with a different reality behind closed doors. When I was a girl, I didn't realize the importance of good oral hygiene. I didn't know I should brush my teeth twice a day. Somehow, I missed that memo. When I noticed that teeth brushing should happen twice daily I started to emulate that. When you emulate good things, you aren't being fake. It means you are bringing the best things into your lives.

I say we are all making it up as we go along, and it's okay that there is a gap between where we are and where we want to be. There is a gap between what we know to be true and our ability to live it. For example, flossing (apparently, I am on an oral hygiene kick). You may know flossing is the best thing to prevent cavities. You may recognize that truth and even tout its importance. But maybe you don't floss daily. Maybe it is rare that you floss at all. But you know it's true and you try to do better.

This isn't hypocrisy. This is you closing the gap between what you know to be true and your ability to live it. There is no shame in that. You will not be able to walk in your true space on this planet if you don't feel congruent with yourself.

Hiding and shame can affect our confidence because we feel we are not being our true selves. When we recognize the need to be vulnerable in select situations to address our shame, we can move forward and walk confidently among others knowing that we are all closing the gap.

In Other(s) Words

"Our stories are not meant for everyone. Hearing them is a privilege, and we should always ask ourselves this before we share: "Who has earned the right to hear my story?" If we have one or two people in our lives who can sit with us and hold space for our shame stories, and love us for our strengths and struggles, we are incredibly lucky. If we have a friend, or small group of friends, or family who embraces our imperfections, vulnerabilities, and power, and fills us with a sense of belonging, we are incredibly lucky."
— Brené Brown

"If we can share our story with someone who responds with empathy and understanding, shame can't survive."
— Brené Brown

"We're never so vulnerable than when we trust someone - but paradoxically, if we cannot trust, neither can we find love or joy."
— Frank Crane

"Owning our story can be hard but not nearly as difficult as spending our lives running from it. Embracing our vulnerabilities is risky but not nearly as dangerous as giving up on love and belonging and joy—the experiences that make us the most vulnerable. Only when we are brave enough to explore the darkness will we discover the infinite power of our light."
— Brené Brown

"Shame corrodes the very part of us that believes we are capable of change."
— Brené Brown
(If you haven't noticed, Brene' Brown is kind of the Queen of Vulnerability and Shame..)

Helping Others

Be that listening ear and the safe place for others to be vulnerable. Validate others that even despite their X that they are worthy of your friendship. Be the receiver that you would want to have with your vulnerability.

Ed(you)cation

Shame Slayers, the best way to slay shame is through vulnerability, even if it is scary to be vulnerable. Share your X with someone so it doesn't swallow you up. Sometimes you have to call in disaster control and get help with things that happen that we have no control over. Sometimes you just need to reach out and air out.

Identify what your X is. Pick someone who is safe to share it with. It will be scary and you will feel vulnerable, but this exercise has power to help you connect with your confident self. If your shame seems so big, too difficult to unpack, maybe you need to call in an expert.

JOURNAL

You build on failure. You use it as a stepping stone. Close the door on the past. You don't try to forget the mistakes, but you don't dwell on it. You don't let it have any of your energy, or any of your time, or any of your space.
--Johnny Cash

MAKING MISTAKES

Newsflash: we all screw up! Not just little things, either. Sometimes we make huge mistakes that change our lives, our relationships, and even our character. The mistakes we make can be difficult to recover from. Sometimes it takes years to get back on track after mistakes, and some choices take us on an entirely different course.

Not being able to move on from our past decisions can be a huge hurdle to our confidence. Especially if our negative self-talk likes to drudge up the past. Mistakes can't be avoided, we are all bumping around on the planet trying our best, making mistakes, and trying again.

I want to share with you a tool I have used to help me move forward after making mistakes. These phrases can be incredibly healing for all involved. I call it *Five Phrases of a Better Apology*. These five phrases can be used when we need to apologize to another person, or they can be used to apologize to yourself.

I learned four of these phrases from the blog, cuppacocoa.com. The writer shared four things in "A Better Way to Say Sorry" that she learned at a teacher's conference that she would have her students say in their community classroom whenever they had wronged a classmate. I thought these suggestions were so good I started using them in my family, and I quickly added a phrase I felt was missing.

Here are the phrases; You don't have to say them exactly as they are listed here, but the spirit behind each phrase is important.

1. I am sorry for...

It is important to get specific and exact in our apology. It reminds me of two kids fighting and the mom forces one child to say sorry. The child says, "I am sorry you're so stupid." instead of saying, "I am sorry I said you were stupid." This slightly humorous example reminds us that being specific is important, both for the person receiving the apology and the person giving it.

2. It was wrong because...

This step allows you to put the offensive choice in context of why the action may have been hurtful, harmful, or simply was not a good choice. This acknowledgment also validates the receiver.

3. Next time, I will...

This phrase is beautiful. It allows us to see that there are different courses of action we can choose in the future to keep us from making the same decision.

I added this step:
4. What can I do to make it right? Or I would like to make it right.

Restitution is healing for both parties. Once my son hurt his friend while they were jumping on a trampoline, when he asked his friend how he could make it right his friend replied that a massage would make him feel better. And it did!

5. Will you forgive me?

This question empowers the person who was wronged by acknowledging they have the option to forgive. It also gives both parties an opportunity for closure.

If you think about each of these statements, you may realize, their power, as I did. I encourage you to try to use them in your life. Again, they don't have to be so rote, however within a few sentences you can easily capture their essence. These phrases help at work, in marriage, with children, siblings, neighbors, and even strangers.

A little side note here: if someone apologizes to you, please do not say, "It's okay." It isn't simply okay, because you don't want them to do it again. Plus, if someone feels the need to apologize and you diminish it with "it's okay," then you diminish them as well. However, sometimes we get apologies and we don't really have enough time to process through them to give a suitable response. Try something like, "Thank you for taking time to apologize," or "Thank you for apologizing, and I would like to think on this for a bit." Then you can have the chance to think about what they said and extend forgiveness at another time. When you do forgive someone, it is nice to say, "I forgive you." Sometimes you can even respond with your own apology if you had a part in the situation.

Another tool I find helpful to move on from mistakes (either our own, or another's) is the Hawaiian reconciliation phrases of Ho'oponopono. They were taught to me by my friend Laura Sonderegger of getrealhealing.com, but their origins are found deep in Hawaiian and Polynesian traditions.

These are the phrases:
I am sorry.
Please forgive me.
Thank you.
I love you.

You can say these phrases to yourself or to someone you have wronged. I love the third phrase, Thank you. We are all making it up as we go along, and when we learn better we do better. Thank you is always about being grateful for lessons learned from our experience. Even in poor choices, there are lessons to help us to choose differently in the future.

In Other(s) Words

"By seeking and blundering we learn."
— Johann Wolfgang von Goethe

"To err is human, to forgive, divine."
— Alexander Pope, An Essay on Criticism

"True forgiveness is when you can say, 'Thank you for that experience'."
— Oprah Winfrey

"When you forgive, you in no way change the past-- but you sure do change the future."
-Bernard Meltzer

Insight of God

I have found the Five Phrases of a Better Apology mentioned earlier to be extremely helpful as I have prayed for forgiveness. They help me feel like I am ready to lay down past choices and move forward. It is through Jesus Christ that I can be cleansed and renewed. We all make mistakes. For those who believe in Jesus Christ, we have a means to move beyond those mistakes because of His sacrifices.

1 John 1:9 says: If we confess our sins, He is faithful and just to forgive us our sins, and to cleanse us from all unrighteousness.

Helping Others

Teach someone the Five Phrases of a Better Apology. This may help them to move on from their own past mistakes.

Ed(you)cation

Consider some of the mistakes that you want to apologize for. Perhaps the 5 phrases need to be shared with that person, either in person, in a letter, or maybe you just need to seek forgiveness over it from yourself. Write down the 5 phrases of a better apology with the specifics of the situation. It is healing.

JOURNAL

"Keep every promise you make and only make promises you can keep."
-- Anthony Hitt

SELF-PROMISES

Lately, I have been pondering quite a bit on self-mastery as it relates to self-confidence.

Confidence is defined by Google thusly (yes, I just threw down thusly): the feeling or belief that one can rely on someone or something; firm trust.

To be self-confident is to trust in one's self, that you can rely on you.

Can you be relied on to do what you say you are going to do? Some of us would never dream of letting anyone else down, but we may find ourselves making promises (large or small) to ourselves that we don't follow through on.

"I am going to quit drinking diet soda."
"I will start waking up early on Monday."
"I will floss nightly."
"I will turn in by nine p.m."
"I will only say kind things about others."
(…insert New Year's resolutions here…)

Perhaps you break promises to yourself because no one is around to witness the promises you make in our head. When the task you promised becomes difficult, you can easily and quickly justify not doing it. Convincing yourself that you should have never made the promise to begin with.

I think that self-trust is like a muscle: the more you exercise it, the stronger it gets. However, the same is true in the inverse, that the more frequently you fail or break your word to yourself, the easier it will be to do it again. When you don't follow through with your self-promises, you lose self-confidence.

Can you see how your esteem of self would be affected by not following through on what you say you will do? I think it leaves us with two choices: either stop making promises to yourself altogether, or start strengthening your Mastery Muscle.

I don't really recommend the first choice at all. To stop making self-promises entirely is counterproductive to progress. I can certainly recommend starting with the latter suggestion: strengthening the Mastery Muscle.

I do believe words have power. Therefore, I wholeheartedly suggest only promising yourself things you truly intend to follow through on. It does harm to our self-esteem to make a promise and not follow through. Really stop and think before saying you are going to do something; ask yourself:

Do I intend on following through?

Do I plan on dedicating my capacity and attention to make the promise true?

If the answer is no, then save your words for when you intend to keep your word.

Self-mastery is like any muscle that must be worked for growth. If you find you haven't been keeping promises to yourself, you can begin a training course to start strengthening your trust in yourself that you will keep your word. The following are suggestions of things you can do to start to strengthen your mastery muscle:

1. Identify the times you do keep your self-promises.

It is important to recognize when you have been trustworthy to yourself.

"I said I was going to wake up early, and I did. Way to go, me!"

When we recognize the mastery we are practicing, we gain the strength to master more.

2. Self-mastery can begin with little things.

Instead of telling yourself, "I am never drinking a soda again," try, "I will not have a diet Coke until four o'clock."

As the hours pass, you can congratulate yourself on your stick-to-it-iveness. You would, of course, eventually progress to not having a diet Coke at all in this scenario. Each time we delay gratification, we are winning and strengthening that Mastery Muscle.

3. Team up.

Connect your new promise with a habit you already do regularly. Do push-ups right after you brush your teeth; call Grandma when you are waiting for basketball practice to end; say something positive about yourself every time you walk in the door. By teaming up a new goal with a well-established one, you increase your self-promise strength.

4. Make it real.

Follow some expert advice and let someone else in on this promise, or write the promise down. Even saying the promise out loud makes it more real. This increases the likelihood that you will follow through.

5. Call it how it is.

If you feel yourself wavering or struggling to keep the promise, then say out loud what is happening and give yourself a talkin' to.

"I said I was going to walk the dog every day, and I don't want to, but I KEEP MY SELF-PROMISES."

This may sound ridiculous, but when you get it out of your head and into reality, you can see things with greater clarity.

6. Return and report.

At the end of the day (or the promised time period), report on your progress. Either to those you are accountable to, to the spot you wrote it down, or to yourself out loud,

"I said I was going to wake up at 5 a.m., and I did!"

Do you see that when you follow through with your self-promises, you strengthen self-confidence!

Imagine building your Mastery Muscle to the point where you believe yourself when you proclaim you are going to do something big: quit smoking, start a new business, run a marathon, cut out sugar. Go to Hawaii, become a millionaire. When you can affect change in your own life by keeping self-promises, your confidence increases. You feel like you are in command of your own life, and that awareness is empowering. You deserve to trust you. You are worth keeping promises to.

In Other(s) Words

"What you get by achieving your goals is not as important as what you become by achieving your goals."
- Zig Ziglar

"Promises are like crying babies in a theater, they should be carried out at once."
- Norman Vincent Peale

"Promises are the uniquely human way of ordering the future, making it predictable and reliable to the extent that this is humanly possible."
-Hannah Arendt

"Some people don't understand the promises they're making when they make them," I said.

"Right, of course. But you keep the promise anyway. That's what love is. Love is keeping the promise anyway."
— John Green, The Fault in Our Stars

Insight of God

Deuteronomy 23:23 says, That which is gone out of thy lips thou shalt keep and perform.

One thing I have also believed is that Jesus gave us the "Holy Spirit of Promise" (Ephesians 1:13), so that we might know that His promises are sure through His Holy Spirit. In the Gospel of Kayla-Leah, I believe we can also ask (as in, ask and ye shall receive--John 16:24) for help in keeping our own promises, that the Holy Spirit of Promise can help us. I believe we can ask for help keeping the commandments to be honest with ourselves and what we say we will do.

Helping Others

Be willing to be an accountability partner for someone else. Follow through when someone has shared a goal with you. Ask them about their progress and teach them any tips you have gained from keeping your word to yourself.

Ed(you)cation

What self-goals or promises are you actively working on right now?

_____

_____

_____

Do you need to write down any self-promises to help you keep your word to yourself?

_____

_____

_____

What was the last promise you fulfilled to yourself? Think about how it made you feel.

_____

_____

_____

Put a star next to any of the tips above that you believe will help you exercise your self-promise muscle.

JOURNAL

"Never bend your head. Always hold it high. Look the world straight in the face."
— *Helen Keller*

CONFIDENCE HAS A POSTURE

I love TED talks. If you don't know what they are, Google TED talks or find it on YouTube. TED is a platform where people share ideas. These are 18 minute talks on an idea that was worth spreading. Topics range from personal development to tech ideas, geology to sociology. You can find a TED talk on any topic you have interest in and topics you didn't even know you were interested in. I find them fascinating and enlightening.

One of my favorite TED talks was by Amy Cuddy. She shared some concepts about body postures and how they affect our self-confidence. The premise of her TED talk shared her research as a social psychologist at Harvard Business School.

According to Amy, when we are feeling insecure, our body shows it. We usually make ourselves smaller than the people around us. We use protective positions, such as covering our heart or throat with our hands and crossing our arms in front of us. If we are sitting, we cross our legs. Our shoulders roll forward and our back hunches to make us shorter. This is what is happening on the outside of our body.

Meanwhile, on the inside we feel like we lack confidence. Our testosterone (the hormone that makes us feel like we can conquer the world) is low and our cortisol (the hormone that puts our body into a stress response) is high.

When we are feeling confident and secure, we also show it in our body language. We physically try to take up as much space as possible: our chest is open, our shoulders are back, our heads are held high. We often will sit with our legs open (this does not apply when sitting with a skirt on!) We will even put our elbow out on the top of the chair, or if we are standing we will have our feet wider than our hips, and perhaps we even place our hands on our hips. Our testosterone levels become elevated (we can conquer the world!) and our cortisol is low (I'm not stressed!).

In Amy Cuddy's TED talk, she shares with us the research that when we feel insecure or confident, our bodies go into these positions and our hormones change. But the inverse is also true. When we hold an insecure body position, our mind reacts the same, whether or not insecure feelings preceded it. We get a boost of cortisol and a decrease in testosterone.

So, strike a confident pose! (Think Wonder Woman, here.) Hands on hips, shoulders back, head high, feet wider than hips. As you're standing, your brain is raising your testosterone (I can conquer the world!) and lowers your cortisol (and I am pretty relaxed about it!).

Cuddy's study shows that if you hold either a secure or insecure pose for 2.5 minutes, it has the power to affect these hormone levels in your body. Her conclusion: you can actually fake confidence until you are confident!

I don't suggest fake-it-till-you-make-it as a long-term strategy when it comes to confidence. I do suggest that you use this technique to give you a boost of confidence in situations that require more self-assurance, such as job interviews, competitions, ceremonies, recitals, first dates, raise negotiations, tests, before overthrowing a dictatorship, or while tending to small children.

When I pitched my idea worth sharing to the TEDx board, I held a confident pose in my car as I drove to the interview. In the elevator, I held a Wonder Woman power pose and as I sat in the lobby I put my shoulder and elbow up on the edge of my chair. This was all done with the intent that it would reinforce my confidence. When I walked in to share my idea I felt confident, composed, and prepared to deliver my

114

content. Whenever I hold confident poses, I feel a difference inside and out.

In addition to great chemical boosts to your confidence, your body posture also tells the world how you feel about yourself. If someone was at a party and feeling insecure, they might shrink, crossing their arms, and finding themselves in the corner. They put up a barrier and it sends a message that they are not comfortable talking to others. Other party-goers are discouraged from approaching the person, becoming a self-fulfilling prophecy: the individual doesn't feel approachable, so they put out signals of unapproachability, and then they leave the party wondering why no one wanted to talk to them.

When you walk through this world with your head held high, your shoulders back, your chest open and with a smile on your face, you are broadcasting a message. You are telling the world you are open to new things and you are open to the goodness available to you. Others will want to be a part of that openness and good feelings, making it easy for them to approach you.

The next time you are trying something new, or want to come across as prepared and confident as you know you are, hold a confident posture and watch the magic happen.

Helping Others

Practice power poses with others when they are preparing for their next big thing. You can even laugh and smile (added bonus!) while you do it. While you power pose, you can teach them all about Amy Cuddy and her research.

In Other(s) Words

"This is it. The darkest day. The blackest hour. Chin up, shoulders back. Let's see what we're made of, you and I."
-The Doctor

"Body language is a very powerful tool. We had body language before we had speech, and apparently, 80% of what you understand in a conversation is read through the body, not the words."
- Deborah Bull

"People assume their confidence is coming from their own thoughts. They don't realize their posture is affecting how much they believe in what they're thinking,"
- Richard Petty

Ed(you)cation

Hold a confident posture for 2.5 minutes. Make it big: head held high, shoulders back, hands on hips, feet wider than your hips. You can even nod your head while thinking, "I have got this!" How does this make you feel? Challenge family and friends to do it with you.

Go people-watching at a mall or at a public event. Just observe body postures of the passers-by. Who is confident? Who is insecure? Who is faking confidence in hopes that their feelings will catch up? The more you observe confident and insecure postures, the more you will be aware of your own. You will be able to use posture to increase your confidence.

JOURNAL

*"Always be a first rate version of yourself and
not a second rate version of someone else."*
— Judy Garland

PRINCIPLES AND PRACTICES

Having fun being you happens when you find specific practices you love to fulfill principles. We sometimes get principles and practices mixed up, and perhaps I can clarify.

A principle is a truth or system of belief, and the practice is the application of that belief. There are often many different practices for a principle.

Let's take the principle of good physical health or fitness. We may believe in good physical fitness, but our practices in achieving fitness vary:

Bootcamp   CrossFit
Running   Yoga
Pilates   Jazzercise
Swimming   Cycling
Jogging   Speed walking
Tennis   Soccer
Weight lifting   Walking the mall
Kick boxing   Zumba
Shine dance   Exercise DVDs
Classes

Do you see all these various practices you can use for principle of achieving physical health? I am quite positive there are even more I haven't mentioned. Did you know there is Yoga with Goats for example? It is true.

All of these examples are different practices. If your girlfriend is knocking it out of the park with spinning and is seeing amazing results, you may try spinning only to find you hate it. Don't be confused and think you hate fitness altogether! Maybe you just need to find a different practice for that principle; don't throw the principle out with the practice. Or the baby with the bathwater. Test out a different practice--it may be different than your girlfriend's. Who knows, maybe hula hooping is your thing!

When you dial into the practice that fits you best, you are going to find more success in the principle. Think of some other principles and practices in your life: are you being true to you in the practices?

If you believe in the principle of having a family meal each night, then what do the practices look like to make it happen? It can happen many different ways, using different practices.

For me, I discovered I have a difficult time finding "I don't care" at the grocery store. That seems to be all my family wants to eat. Well, occasionally they request "whatever," but I don't know how to cook that. In other words, I have a hard time coming up with meal plans. I don't really get much joy out of cooking. I like the principle of having a family meal each night, but I don't like the practice that requires me to plan and prepare every meal.

I do, on the other hand, love the practice we've adopted where each individual member of my family has to come up with one meal idea and help to prepare that meal (with my help) on their assigned day. It is a win for everyone. I don't have to plan meals on my own, my children get to learn how to cook, and they get to have a say in what we eat. Win, Win, Win.

Let me share some laundry practices. One time I told my son that he needed to change his shirt. It was his favorite and he had worn it for too many days in a row. He began crying (he was seven at the time).

120

Through his tears, he protested, "If I put it in the wash, I won't see it for a week! Why can't you do the laundry all in one day like Zac's mom?!"

Clearly Zac's mom has a different practice than I did, and I have made a few adjustments to my practices over the years. I still don't have a one-day turnaround on everything, but sometimes you have to make a just few tweaks to get it just right.

Do you hang the clothes or fold them for drawers? Do you put the clothes away or do the kiddos? Where do your socks live? The underwear?

Finding practices that spark the most joy for you is crucial! Maybe laundry isn't so fun, but I do like to use fabric softener and those smell good crystals. I also like how I can stand at the dryer and have everything in my reach to sort hang, fold, and stack all of the different types of laundry we have in our house. The principle of having clean clothes for my family does spark joy. I have found some practices that spark joy as well.

Sometimes I struggle with sitting still, which makes helping my kiddos with homework seem really, really, really boring. I try to mix up the practices by throwing in different techniques, like using a dry erase marker on the fridge or window, basketball spelling where we dribble for each letter, flash cards as a race against dad, and funny songs to help us remember things. I believe in the principle of teaching my kiddos, and I also believe the more fun you have in the practice the more likely it will get done, and ultimately, the more your children will learn.

Sometimes, unfortunately, we emulate someone else's practice when we mean to emulate their principles.

I have a dear friend who is a phenomenal house keeper. (She is also quite proficient at dinner.) For the longest time, I wanted to be just like her, until I realized that I couldn't be Amy Robinson because I wouldn't have enough time to be Kayla-Leah. I couldn't keep her house cleaning schedule because I had twice as many kiddos that were half the ages of hers. She and I also had different practices for our service, our outlets of creativity, occupations, and different family demands.

I wanted to emulate the principles of having a clean and welcoming home, and I learned that I get to be in charge of what that looked like for me. And so do you! As it turns out, you are the CEO of your life. I found the practices of housekeeping that fit my family.

I want to share with you the concept of "OR". It looks like this:

A friend of mine was once working with a writing coach. She was writing twelve minutes a day using assigned writing prompts. One day she complained that she didn't want to write about the prompt she was given that day--she wanted to write about something else. I reminded her, "You could write about the prompt, _or_ keep the principle of twelve minutes, while writing what you want."

Here are a few other "_or_" choices:

I could go to boot camp, _or_ I could go play indoor soccer, which I love. I could make dinner, _or_ I could delegate to others the task of making dinner.
I could clean my house completely in one day, _or_ I could do a little each day.

There is value in evaluating the principles and practices at play in your life. When you find practices that bring you joy, you can be more confident when you see others choosing different principles and practices than your own.

In Other(s) Words

"Follow your inner moonlight; don't hide the madness."
— Allen Ginsberg

"A girl should be two things: who and what she wants."
— Coco Chanel

"There is a vitality, a life force, an energy, a quickening that is translated through you into action, and because there is only one of you in all time, this expression is unique. And if you block it, it will never exist through any other medium and will be lost."
— Martha Graham

Helping Others

Often, you are in the position to see what's hiding in the blind spots of those around you. If you see someone struggling with a practice while growing frustrated at the principle, you can offer a fresh perspective and give them ideas on how to change the practice and not abandon the principle. There may be resistance to suggestions, you can always make them and follow up with, "You know you best, and I am sure you can find a way to still make this work, but maybe with a different approach."

Ed(you)cation

What are some of the principles and practices in your own life?
What do you do to practice fitness?
What service practices do you have?
What is your laundry practice?
What are your money and finance principles and practices?
If quality family time is your principle, what are your practices to make it happen?
What are your worship practices?
How do you practice the principle of connection?
Which practices spark joy?
Which practices don't spark joy?
What practices can be changed or tweaked to spark more joy?

JOURNAL

"Stay afraid, but do it anyway. What's important is the action. You don't have to wait to be confident. Just do it and eventually the confidence will follow."
--Carrie Fisher

FEAR FACTOR

I was speaking at a women's retreat and knew that one of the planned activities was a zip-line in the Idaho mountains.

I hate heights.

I have attempted to overcome this fear many times in my life. Once, I naively convinced myself that if I jumped out of an airplane at 15,000 feet, I would never fear heights again. First off, I didn't get to jump out of an airplane. I had to crawl out onto the wing and hold on to a brace, getting in position before I let go. I had my eyes closed for most of the free fall, and I panicked when the tandem flyer on my back released some of the tension in the gear that held us together, despite his assurances that I would not come unlatched from him. After I relaxed I found that skydiving was beautiful, exhilarating, and fun. The closer I got to the ground, however, the more I became aware of how high we were. My fear of being so high returned in full force. That was nearly fifteen years ago, and my fear of heights has not diminished.

At this more recent women's retreat, I was determined to do the zip-line. I just didn't know how I was going to do it and keep my dignity.

We lined up near the platform on the top of the mountainside. The camp director had designed the zip-line challenge around a theme:

"Let it Go". Each participant wrote on a water balloon something we needed to "let go," and as we approached the landing of the zip-line we were to release our water balloons and attempt to get it in a trash can.

One by one, my fellow campers chose something they wanted to let go of. Things like shame, extra weight, judgement. On my water balloon, I wrote FEAR. Again, I thought, if I could survive the zip-line, my fear of heights would leave me for good.

Luckily, there were several campers ahead of me in line, and I had plenty of time to ponder on my fear of heights and how I was going to "let go."

I first thought about why I wanted to overcome this fear. There is nothing wrong with fearing heights, I reasoned. Lots of people fear heights. I could easily strive to avoid heights the rest of my life. And then… I remembered a family camping trip just a month before.

My family loves to camp, and we do a ton of activities when we are camping. We love being active together. Sometimes when we camp, my family goes rappelling or cliff diving. I don't join in, but I am usually right at the bottom of the cliff and can watch as they rappel down. Or I am swimming in the water as my boys and husband climb the rocks to jump in.

Every year we hike through a river canyon going bouldering, where we hike to a waterfall and then end up at some hot springs. It is my favorite activity. This year, instead of entering the canyon at our designated spot, my father and family decided to rappel in off this 200-foot cliff, which was a quicker route to the waterfall and hot springs.

Because of my fear of heights, I watched as each one of them went over the edge, all the way from my sixty-three-year-old father to my nine-year-old son. I watched as two of my boys, scared to the point of shaking, still chose to go over the edge. After they rappelled down, I got in the jeep and set off to pick them up.

I felt left behind because I had missed out on the adventure. They were enjoying the bouldering, waterfall, and experience without me. I let fear get in the way of doing something with my family. The longer I pondered on this, the more determined I became to overcome this fear.

Then I realized that this fear of heights may never go away. But having courage is not never feeling fear; courage is feeling fear but not letting fear keep you from progressing.

What helped me run down the platform to zip across the canyon was to focus on my why instead of my fear. My why was my family. My boys--to do things as a family to create fun and memories.

I focused on my why and guess what??? Flying down that zip-line was a piece of cake. When I got down on the ground I called my husband and told him I needed to start rappelling so I could be ready for next year's canyon rappel and waterfall trip.

Fear comes in many forms. Fear of heights, speaking, failure. I believe that all of them can be conquered by focusing on your why. Perhaps your fear, like mine, is one that will have to be faced again and again. It may never completely go away or it may ease with time, but the approach is the same.

Your fear of speaking can be overcome when you focus on the why behind your message. Your fear of failure can be overcome when you focus on why you need success. Confidence and courage are similar: you may still have fear while living confidently and acting courageously. Don't run from your fears--embrace them, dance with them. Take action.

The guide who prepared us for the zip-line shared some advice that I had found to be helpful. He suggested we imagine concentric circles on the ground. The inner circle is your comfort zone. This is where we like to stay, but staying there doesn't challenge us and it doesn't scare us. This zone is the most comfortable.

The very outer circle is terrifying fear. This is where you are so afraid you feel like you could actually die. All sorts of sections of your brain shut down, paralyzed. You would experience this kind of fear if you were going over a waterfall in a barrel.

Then there is a circle between the innermost comfortable circle and the outermost fearful circle. In the middle circle, we experience fear, but it's also the zone where we can experience the most growth. This middle zone is called growth.

When we want to try something new we usually have to leave that inner comfort zone and step out into the uncomfortable and fearful. So, why do we do it? Because that is where we will find growth. We actually gain confidence when we try new things, which may seem counterintuitive. Why would we grow more confident doing something we don't know, that we have never done, that we may fail at, or be awkward at? The reason is the process strengthens our growth muscles and when there is growth there is success. When you feel success your confidence soars! Living our lives in this middle circle may not look pretty and it certainly won't look perfect, but it does bring growth.

If you need the courage and confidence to take that step outside your inner comfort zone, just remember your why.

My family got together to discuss a family motto recently, and there were many ideas being tossed around. (Now, I don't want you to get the false notion that four boys, including three teens, joyfully participated in this activity with enthusiasm and are now eager to embrace our new motto. They were resistant, reluctant, and still really do not yet see my vision.) Nevertheless, we came up with a motto that we are working on embracing.

The Rich family motto is: JUST GO AND DO!

Thanksgiving morning came along this year shortly after we created our motto. We examined our options of stretching our stomachs with a big breakfast or we could go hiking at Table Rock (a favorite local hike overlooking the city). I groaned slightly at the latter suggestion and then I thought to myself, "Just go and do!" We ended up hiking, and the excursion was pure happiness.

Do you need to wake up at 5:30 in the morning to keep the rest of your day in balance? Just Go and Do! Time to go back to school? Just Go and Do!

Perhaps you can borrow our family motto until you find one of your own.

Square Dancing? Just Go and Do!

Glass Blowing? Just Go and Do!

Goat Yoga? Just...don't, that would just be weird.

Unless...well, if you want to... Just Go and Do!

Try new things. It takes you out of your comfort zone!

Thanks to Wikipedia, I found a great starting list of indoor hobbies followed by a list of outdoor hobbies. I want you to put an X by any of the following you think it would be fun to try or funny to learn. Not that you must do it, but that you think it would be fun to do it. (Look, I went to the trouble of adding the list, please just take a minute to put an X by the things you think would be fun, alright?!)

Indoor Activities

3D printing

Acting

Board games

Cabaret

Candle making

Coffee roasting

Coloring

Couponing

Crocheting

Cryptography

Digital arts

Drawing

Electronics

Fantasy sports

Fishkeeping

Foreign languages

Glassblowing

Homebrewing

Jewelry making

Juggling

Knitting

Knife making

Lapidary

Amateur radio

Baton twirling

Book restoration

Calligraphy

Computer programing

Cooking

Cosplaying

Creative writing

Crossword puzzles

Dance

Drama

DIY decorating

Embroidery

Fashion

Flower arranging

Genealogy

Gunsmithing

Iceskating

Jigsaw puzzles

Knapping

Kabaddi

Lacemaking

Lego building

Lockpicking
Machining
Metalworking
Model building
Painting
Pottery
Quilting
Scrapbooking
Sewing
Sketching
Stand up comedy
Table tennis
Video gaming
Whittling
Wood carving
Writing

Lucid dreaming
Macrame
Magic
Origami
Poi
Puzzles
Reading
Sculpting
Singing
Soapmaking
Tatting
Taxidermy
Watching movies
Wikipedia editing
World building
Yoga

Outdoor Hobbies
Archery
Base jumping
Basketball
Bird watching
Board sports
Brazilian jiu-jitsu
Dowsing
Fishing
Flying
Foraging
Geocaching
Graffiti (really, Wikipedia?)
Hiking
Horseback riding
Inline skating
Kayaking
Kite surfing
Letterboxing
Motor sports
Mountaineering
Netball
Orienteering

Astronomy
Baseball
Beekeeping
Blacksmithing
Body building
Camping
Driving
Flag football
Flying disc
Gardening
Ghost hunting
Handball
Hooping
Hunting
Logging
Kite flying
LARPing (Google it)
Metal detection
Mountain biking
Mushroom hunting
Nordic skating
Paintball

Parkour

Polo

Rappelling

Rock climbing

Rugby

Sailing

Scouting

Sculling

Shooting

Skateboarding

Skim Boarding

Slacklining

Soccer

Surfing

Taekwondo

Urban Exploration

Vehicle Restoration

Water sports

Photography

Rafting

Road biking

Roller skating

Running

Sand art

Scuba diving

Topiary

Shopping

Skiing

Skydiving

Snowboarding

Stone skipping

Swimming

Tai Chi

Vacation

Walking

By trying new things, you get out of your comfort zone and into growth. It allows you to find new activities that "Spark Joy." It helps you live life to its fullest. It is worth taking that first step out of your inner circle.

This list includes many fun and interesting hobbies, many of which will take courage to try. I know that beyond trying new things, you also have to face some large fears in life, such as new jobs, changes in relationships, and health issues. The antidote to fear is the same for each: focus on the "Why" and take action.

In Other(s) Words

"Courage is being scared to death and saddling up anyway."
- John Wayne

"Thinking will not overcome fear but action will."
— W. Clement Stone

"The amateur believes he must first overcome his fear; then he can do his work. The professional knows that fear can never be overcome. He knows there is no such thing as a fearless warrior or a dread-free artist."
–Steven Pressfield

"Action is a great restorer and builder of confidence. Inaction is not only the result, but the cause, of fear. Perhaps the action you take will be successful; perhaps different action or adjustments will have to follow. But any action is better than no action at all."
— Norman Vincent Peale

"I will not die an unlived life. I will not live in fear of falling or catching fire. I choose to inhabit my days, to allow my living to open me, to make me less afraid, more accessible, to loosen my heart until it becomes a wing, a torch, a promise. I choose to risk my significance; to live so that which comes to me as seed goes to the next as blossom and that which comes to me as blossom, goes on as fruit."
— Dawna Markova

Helping Others

You are the "why reminder". When you see someone in their comfort zone but longing to move into growth, remind them of their why to help them overcome their fear.

Ed(you)cation

What are some activities that you have always wanted to try but were too scared?

Are there things your friends or family do that you won't participate in?

What are some of your fears?

What could happen if you fail? What could happen if you succeed?

List any "whys" that could help you overcome fear.

From the list of activities on the previous pages, pick four activities that you put an X by. Google that activity. See what is involved and watch others do it. Just for fun and a little learning!

Try one of the activities that you haven't tried before.

JOURNAL

_____

_____
_____
_____
_____
_____
_____
_____
_____
_____
_____
_____
_____
_____
_____
_____
_____
_____
_____
_____
_____
_____
_____
_____
_____
_____
_____
_____

"No one has ever become poor by giving."
— Anne Frank

BEING A BUCKET FILLER

I first came across the concept of being a Bucket Filler by reading a book in a grade school classroom. The concept is this: everyone is walking around holding an invisible bucket. When we interact with each other, we either fill their bucket or we deplete their bucket. Kind words fill buckets, mean words deplete. Thoughtful actions, bucket fillers; selfish actions, bucket drainers. The most interesting part is that when we work on filling other's buckets, we also fill our own. When we draw from other's buckets, we draw down our own. This is a universal truth in my opinion.

I often play a game in Walmart. I walk up and down the aisles making eye contact and smiling at strangers. Sometimes I even say hello or give them a compliment. The responses I get are always surprising. I think sometimes people respond in kind before they realize what they have done. Smiles are contagious. A smile begets a smile which is awesome. Playing smile tag feels amazing.

"On a biochemical level, smiling releases endorphins and serotonin. Endorphins are natural painkillers. The more endorphins your brain releases, the more your body can fight off symptoms of illness. Similarly, serotonin is a brain chemical that acts as a natural anti-depressant. Reshaping our mouth from a frown to a smile literally sparks serotonins, dramatically shifting our sense of well-being from negative to positive." (8)

If you go around smiling at others, their natural instinct is to return that smile with another smile. This is literally spreading happiness, filling their bucket and yours in return.

I have never played this game and lost. I always feel amazing when I engage others and develop a connection with a smile. This is the easiest way to be a bucket filler!

I have always heard that if you want to find yourself, you should lose yourself in service. One of the key strategies to building confidence is to give service. Be intentional about the service you give, and select the service that sparks the most joy. You may consider working at a homeless shelter or an animal shelter; perhaps teaching a child to read, sitting with the elderly, picking up trash in the foothills of your community, sorting food at a pantry, or teaching computer skills to refugees. There are countless ways to provide service around us! When you pick an opportunity that aligns with your interests or talents, everyone wins.

Something amazing happens to your confidence when you take your time, talents, and energy to serve someone else. It fills up your bucket while it fills theirs. It gives life a sense of purpose when we focus outward instead of inward. Many people search their whole life for a sense of purpose and giving service is the answer.

Service opens new opportunities. Many success stories begin with a door opening using the key of service. Some of my personal dreams of being a speaker and reaching a variety of audiences happened when I took my eye off that prize and focused on giving service. For example, for years I have aspired to give a TED talk, but the topic just wasn't there. When I said yes to the opportunity to go to Haiti and do service, and continued that service when I returned home through Days For Girls, then the topic emerged through that service.

One of the resources I use to find service opportunities is the website justserve.org. I love it because you can type in your zip code and find opportunities in your own town. You can even find something for the same day, one-time service, or service on a regular basis.

Being intentional about serving family members and friends is another way to fill your bucket. Service strengthens these relationships, which in turn helps you to feel more loved and supported. Finding secret ways to serve is a lot of fun.

One easy way to fill someone else's bucket is to write a letter of encouragement. Sending it anonymously makes it an even more beautiful gift. I had a friend once who received a card in the mail; the sender conveyed how impressed they were by how well she was doing as a mom. It was unsigned. My friend went about her day thinking maybe it was from a neighbor, someone from work, church, or school. It could have been sent by anyone, so in a small way it seemed as though everyone could be thinking she was doing a great job.

In addition to filling other's buckets there are other ways to fill your own bucket. It is important to have a full bucket for happiness, and so you are not so depleted that it is difficult to give to others. It comes in the form of coloring with your purple crayons (the things that Spark Joy for you).

Some of my Purple Crayons look like:
Enjoying a book by the fire with hot cocoa.
Watching America's Funniest Videos with my kiddos.
Visiting on the phone with a friend.
Polishing my toes in a bright color.
Watching a British period piece on Netflix.
Creating art with fabric.

A small note about being a bucket filler: although helping fill someone else's bucket is a noble desire, it's not our responsibility to make sure another person's bucket is full all the time. The only bucket we need to focus on filling to the top is our own. I mention this because sometimes people around us have holes in their buckets; you can fill and fill and fill but until they fix the holes, their bucket may become depleted faster than you can fill it. And you can't repair their holes for them. You can only work on repairing any holes in your own bucket.

Perhaps you feel like there are holes in your bucket that need repaired for you to feel filled by service. Fixing holes takes time, and often require help to repair. Repairs take intention, they may take part-nering with a life coach or counselor. In the meantime, keep serving and filling your bucket. This will bring you Joy as you work on mending the holes.

In Other(s) Words

"The best way to find yourself is to lose yourself in the service of others."
— Mahatma Gandhi

"At the end of life we will not be judged by how many diplomas we have received, how much money we have made, how many great things we have done. We will be judged by 'I was hungry, and you gave me something to eat, I was naked and you clothed me. I was homeless, and you took me in.'"
— Mother Teresa

"I slept and dreamt that life was joy. I awoke and saw that life was service. I acted and behold, service was joy."
— Rabindranath Tagore

Helping Others

Engage others in doing service activities. It is much easier to do service in pairs. If you have friend or family member who is struggling, find a way for them to do some service with you.

Insight of God

I love the New Testament example of what it means when we serve others. In Matthew 25:34-40 we read,

Then shall the King say unto them on his right hand, Come, ye blessed of my Father, inherit the kingdom prepared for you from the foundation of the world:
For I was hungred, and ye gave me meat: I was thirsty, and ye gave me drink: I was a stranger, and ye took me in:
Naked, and ye clothed me: I was sick, and ye visited me: I was in prison, and ye came unto me.

Then shall the righteous answer him, saying, Lord, when saw we thee and hungered, and fed thee? or thirsty, and gave thee drink?

When saw we thee a stranger, and took thee in? or naked, and clothed thee?
Or when saw we thee sick, or in prison, and came unto thee?
And the King shall answer and say unto them, Verily I say unto you, Inasmuch as ye have done it unto one of the least of these my brethren, ye have done it unto me.

When we, or others around us, have holes in our happiness buckets, there is a real need to repair those holes so our happiness doesn't flow out faster than it comes in. We need to have a whole container to hold our joy. There are many self-help or personal development practices that attempt to fill our holes, but I believe that to be made whole again we have to go to the Master.

Here are a few scriptures where Jesus Christ made people whole again. Becoming whole again is possible and requires faith.

"And he said unto her, Daughter, be of good comfort: thy faith hath made thee whole; go in peace" (Luke 8:48).

"And immediately the man was made whole, and took up his bed, and walked: and on the same day was the Sabbath" (John 5:9).

I urge you to go to the Master and become whole.

Ed(you)cation

For the next two weeks, look for service opportunities and do them.
List the last service you gave and how it made you feel.
What small ways can you fill someone's bucket?
What ways can you fill your own bucket?

JOURNAL

"Maybe it's NOT Maybelline. Maybe you were just born with it."
— Mandy Hale

CONFIDENCE AND BEAUTY

Forgive me for standing on my soapbox on this chapter, but...

WHO SAYS YOU HAVE TO BE BEAUTIFUL TO DESERVE SPACE ON THIS PLANET?

Yes, I was yelling, and here is why: you have so many qualities that make you unique and amazing! Characteristics that make you worthwhile and worthy. Why must one, particular quality trump everything else?

Of course, there are several multi-million dollar industries designed around lifting beauty up on a pedestal to be the end-all quality to seek after. However, I can think of many traits that have more significance than beauty. For example, being:

• Sincere	• Honest
• Understanding	• Loyal
• Truthful	• Trustworthy
• Intelligent	• Dependable
• Open-Minded	• Thoughtful
• Wise	• Considerate
• Good-Natured	• Reliable
• Mature	• Warm

- Earnest
- Friendly
- Happy
- Interesting
- Good-Humored
- Humorous
- Cheerful
- Warm-Hearted
- Gentle
- Educated
- Companionable
- Trusting
- Pleasant
- Quick-Witted
- Helpful
- Imaginative
- Self-Disciplined
- Enthusiastic
- Polite
- Smart
- Sharp-witted
- Ambitious
- Respectful
- Good-tempered
- Conscientious
- Alert
- Witty
- Kindly
- Patient
- Perceptive
- Sportsmanlike
- Cooperative
- Intellectual
- Capable
- Constructive
- Progressive
- Observant
- Lively
- Punctual
- Prompt

- Kind
- Kind-Hearted
- Clean
- Unselfish
- Honorable
- Responsible
- Trustful
- Broad-Minded
- Well-Spoken
- Reasonable
- Likable
- Clever
- Courteous
- Tactful
- Appreciative
- Outstanding
- Brilliant
- Level-Headed
- Original
- Forgiving
- Well-read
- Bright
- Efficient
- Grateful
- Resourceful
- Good
- Clear-headed
- Admirable
- Talented
- Spirited
- Well-mannered
- Ethical
- Versatile
- Courageous
- Productive
- Individualistic
- Ingenious
- Neat
- Logical
- Accurate

- Sensible
- Self-Reliant
- Amusing
- Generous
- Energetic
- Self-Controlled
- Active
- Respectable
- Wholesome
- Cordial
- Attentive
- Frank
- Decent
- Realist
- Poised
- Realistic
- Optimistic
- Entertaining
- Vivacious
- Relaxed
- Proficient
- Skillful
- Gracious
- Nice
- Skilled
- Modern
- Sociable
- Decisive
- Tidy
- Upright
- Practical
- Well-bred
- Self-confident
- Studious
- Discreet
- Thorough
- Inquisitive
- Outgoing
- Casual
- Moral
- Creative
- Tolerant
- Clean-Cut
- Sympathetic
- High-spirited
- Tender
- Independent
- Inventive
- Congenial
- Experienced
- Cultured
- Purposeful
- Diligent
- Eager
- Competent
- Amiable
- Vigorous
- Adventurous
- Composed
- Romantic
- Rational
- Enterprising
- Able
- Agreeable
- Curious
- Charming
- Modest
- Humble
- Popular
- Literary
- Light-hearted
- Refined
- Cool-headed
- Adventuresome
- Informal
- Exuberant
- Easygoing
- Self-sufficient
- Consistent
- Self-assured

- Untiring
- Calm
- Positive
- Artistic
- Scientific
- Social
- Careful
- Comical
- Religious
- Dignified
- Idealistic
- Disciplined
- Definite
- Persuasive
- Quick
- Thrifty
- Objective
- Righteous
- Meditative
- Systematic
- Daring
- Proud
- Moralistic
- Excited
- Satirical
- Reserved
- Meticulous
- Deliberate
- Bold
- Cautious
- Inoffensive
- Methodical
- Self-contented
- Forward
- Outspoken
- Impulsive
- Conservative
- Unpredictable

- Hopeful
- Strong-minded
- Confident
- Precise
- Orderly
- Direct
- Candid
- Obliging
- Soft-hearted
- Philosophical
- Soft-spoken
- Serious
- Convincing
- Obedient
- Sophisticated
- Sentimental
- Nonconforming
- Mathematical
- Fearless
- Subtle
- Lucky
- Sensitive
- Talkative
- Moderate
- Prudent
- Persistent
- Unconventional
- Painstaking
- Suave
- Innocent
- Shrewd
- Nonchalant
- Perfectionistic
- Excitable
- Quiet
- Changeable
- Shy
- Solemn

(You caught me, I didn't think of all those. I Googled them!) (9)

When I first looked through this list, I thought it listed well-bred (not well-read). I thought, "Are you kidding me?" I had to do a double take, all the while thinking, "What the heck? Well-bred? That isn't a quality we have any control over, and if we did..."

Thankfully, I had just mis-read it. Well-bred would be as out of place in our list as beauty when considering admirable qualities. We have no control over how two sets of DNA intermingled to create our own. We have no control over how certain physical traits have interacted and passed through generations to us.

What is considered beautiful has changed throughout the decades and centuries, even over millennia. Twiggy was once held up as an icon of beauty, then Cindy Crawford and Tyra Banks-- each of these women very different in appearances. Physical traits, such as curves, tan skin, pale skin, or freckles come in and out of vogue. We have no control over if our particular traits happen to be popular at the time we live on the planet.

There are some great campaigns out there redefining beauty. Dove, for example, started a campaign in 2004 about "Real Beauty". Their advertisements show women of all shapes, sizes, ethnicities, and ages. Dove's aim is to show how every woman is beautiful, regardless of her physical traits. I think that Dove's intent is to sell a product while also trying to shape an idea, that we are all beautiful.

My son possesses a unique combination of strengths and struggles, it comes with his Asperger's. He gets very specific when it comes to words. The meaning of words matter deeply to him and if someone uses a word in a way they don't really mean then he sometimes fixates on the difference. I guess I feel the same way about beauty.

Often times, people use the word beauty to define any quality that is valuable, praiseworthy, or desirable to them, when the word originated as a way to describe something aesthetically pleasing. People sometimes say others possess "true beauty" or "real beauty" or "inner beauty" when that's not really what they mean. They are trying to highlight other qualities a person has, but redefine them as "beautiful." In other words, we have held beauty as a standard for so long we are now trying to make other qualities "beautiful." But beauty is the wrong word to use and I think it matters because the over usage of the word keeps beauty as the standard to aim for in everything.

If beauty is defined as a pleasing appearance; a person or thing that is beautiful has perfection of form, color, etc., then beauty is purely an assessment of visual things, and not all qualities can be assessed visually. (10)

You may find yourself to be aesthetically pleasing. If you are, that is one trait.

But what if you are not? What if you have a combination of physical features that are not considered beautiful in this day and age? What is the harm in not being beautiful? Rather than being beautiful, what if you're nurturing, inventive, or spontaneous?

The world tries to redefine beauty by taking other qualities and holding them up as beauty. Someone who is caring is redefined as beautiful; someone who has overcome obstacles is redefined as beautiful. Well-meant intentions aside, this is still placing beauty on a pedestal as the highest and most desirable achievement we can strive for.

But I say, beautiful or not, you have so many other qualities of value that are the foundation of your confidence that beauty is hardly worth mentioning.

Sometimes I am beautiful, but most of the time I am not. But my kindness, positivity, and virtue have no shelf life. They don't change with the times. These qualities allow me to walk with confidence despite the constant barrage and flux of beauty messages. If we lived in some bizarre world where we had to choose between beauty and kindness, beauty and wisdom, beauty and charity, I would choose the latter every time.

Now all of this being said, we each have a container that holds all our goodness; it is our bodies. Your body is only the package, and the greatness is all on the inside! In marketing and sales, the package is really important to entice the consumer to purchase what is in the container. This is important in advertising, but it doesn't apply to humanity! You truly don't have to sell yourself to anyone else to have value. So whether your package is large or small, has a plain wrapper or colorful graphics, the outside is nothing in comparison to what is contained within.

So, does that mean we should forget our package all together?

I want to take care of my body the best I can because it is the vehicle that takes me places. I also like to use my container as a form of self-expression. I love color, so I wear color. I like texture, so I wear texture. (I am not so naïve to think that these multi-million dollar beauty industries have had no influence over me through my life.) However, I do try to remain centered in my true strengths, and I believe those strengths are not known as beauty.

Have fun dressing your package; keep yourself clean. Have fun expressing your personality in your hairstyle and accessories. Or if those things don't spark joy for you, then don't do them! Your outside packaging is the least significant of the qualities you possess. It should be the last quality you spend any time or effort on.

I stream live Facebook videos to share tips and tricks I have picked up over the years. Sometimes I have played with my hair and makeup and clothing, but I often make these videos with no makeup, un-done hair, and even in work-out wear. I do it intentionally to show that you don't have to be all made-up to add value to others. You don't have to be beautiful to do great things.

Beauty does have a way of drawing people to something or someone by being aesthetically pleasing. But if you think beauty has power, try being attractive! I think of being attractive as drawing people to you, like a moth is attracted to a light. Like goodness is attracted to goodness.

Guess what? A smile is attractive, confidence is attractive, joy is attractive, and kindness is attractive. Laughter...you guessed it...attractive! When we attract others to us we can learn, grow, and relate with them.

I have tried to be more aware of the compliments I pay others Instead of telling a little girl she is beautiful, I try to pick a quality she actually has control over. I will tell her she is really observant, or hard working, or giving. This can be hard to remember sometimes, but I want to help the next generation of girls find greater depth in themselves.

With as many messages we receive daily about how wrong, old, fat, or ugly our bodies are, we may struggle to keep our true worth in focus. Remember, you have so many other worthy characteristics that can't be sold in magazines! Focus on all your other qualities, and it won't make a difference to you if beauty is on your list or not.

In Other(s) Words

"It is amazing how complete is the delusion that beauty is goodness."
— Leo Tolstoy, The Kreutzer Sonata

"Beauty isn't worth thinking about; what's important is your mind. You don't want a fifty-dollar haircut on a fifty-cent head."
— Garrison Keillor

"Beauty? To me it is a word without sense because I do not know where its meaning comes from nor where it leads to."
- Pablo Picasso

"If we took selfies of our souls would they be attractive enough to post?"
-Unknown

Helping Others

Make a conscious effort to compliment someone on something other than their beauty. Or if someone has made effort with their package in a new way, mention it but also remind them of other qualities they have that shine even brighter. It could look like this: "Wow, you look great today! You are so artistic when it comes to your clothing and makeup." Or perhaps, "Wow you look great. Your eyes are really inviting--good thing you are so kind to go with it!"

152

Insight of God

1 Samuel 16:7 says, But the Lord said unto Samuel, look not on his countenance, or on the height of his stature...for the Lord seeth not as man seeth; for man looketh on the outward appearance, but the Lord looketh on the heart.

Ed(you)cation

I want you to go back to the list up above (you know, the one you skimmed over) and circle any qualities that you recognize in yourself or any that you are nurturing. I want you to have a good long list to remind yourself that you are so much more than meets the eye.

I am serious...do it! There is power in this exercise.

JOURNAL

"'I'm not a stranger,' I said, and pointed to his book. 'I'm someone who reads the same authors you do.'"
— Lemony Snicket

MEETING NEW PEOPLE:
A COMMON SUGGESTION FOR CONFIDENCE BUILDING

Sometimes I ask my clients if others have suggested ways to build their confidence. I often hear that no one really suggests how to build confidence, except to suggest that they "meet new people."

I think meeting new people is extremely difficult for a lot of us! I can see if you're unprepared, meeting new people can make you feel more insecure than when you started.

I believe the more prepared you are for any situation, the more confident you can become as you go through it.

Perhaps you are an introvert and do not refuel by being out with others. That is okay! You don't have to try to color with gray to make others happy. You don't have to continually seek situations where you meet strangers. However, if you find yourself in social situations and want to be at ease, I suggest you go prepared. The more prepared you are, the more confident you will be. If you know you will be going into a social setting--be it a party, business meeting, networking event, or church gathering--then remember the power poses (Chapter 11). Holding a confident pose before the event can increase your testosterone, lower your cortisol, and give you that extra boost of confidence you need to tackle any situation.

For some, meeting new people comes naturally. For them, it is second nature to strike up conversations with strangers. For those who don't fit this category, I hope to share some tips on meeting new people that will make it easier each time you meet new people.

Posture.

As I mentioned before, holding a confident pose before an event is helpful. Standing in a full Wonder Woman pose once the party or networking event has begun may get you a few curious stares and glances. There are, however, ways you can hold your body that communicates to those around you that you are open to meeting new people. It does not look like this: standing by the wall, clutching your purse or briefcase like a life vest, and your arms folded across your chest.

Most social gatherings offer some sort of food or drink, so having a cup in your hand can ease some nerves. However, do not use it to protect or close off your body. Remember to keep your body as open as possible whether you are sitting or standing, with your shoulders back, head up, making eye contact, and SMILING! This shows others they can comfortably approach you. You can also look around for others who are using their body language to show you they are approachable.

Ice Breakers.

When two people who haven't spoken to each other before try to strike up a conversation, there may seem to be a little resistance. Perhaps it even seems a little chilly. Think about sitting in a waiting room with strangers or on an elevator. Sometimes there is uncomfortable silence, however, once one person "breaks the ice," conversations generally start flowing. Once the ice is broken, our humanity takes over and conversation can begin. Whether it fills the two-minute elevator ride or occupies your time while at a party, there are benefits to reaching out to other human beings. We learn a little something new about ourselves from every person we meet. BE WILLING TO BE THE ICEBREAKER--make the first move!

One safe way you can break the ice is by talking about the weather. As cheesy as this sounds, this tactic generally works. Since weather is a changeable thing, you usually have an easy start.

"Are you surviving this heat?"
"Boy, the weather has been lovely lately."
"Have you been staying warm out there?"
"Are you buried in this snow at your house?"

A follow-up question to the weather might be one concerning geography:

"Have you always lived here?"
"Are you from Boise?" (Insert your city here.)

For women, a compliment on their clothing, shoes, hair, or accessories is usually an excellent conversation starter.

"I love your shoes, such a great brown!"
"Those are great earrings, are they heavy?"

If children are present, asking questions about parenthood, grandparenthood, and the like are also excellent starters. Grandpas love talking about their grandchildren.

"How old is your granddaughter?"
"Is this your only child?"

If you break the ice in the form of a question, then the ball is now in the other person's court to respond. Ninety-nine out of a hundred times, the other person will respond in kind. (Don't worry about that one person who doesn't. Their response is a reflection on them, not you!)

Introductions.

It isn't always necessary to introduce yourself when you're around new people, for example that quick elevator trip. However, at parties, business settings, or other gatherings, be prepared to introduce yourself. It also doesn't hurt to add a tid-bit about you in the introduction to get a conversation started. It can look like this:

"Hi, my name is Kayla Rich." (Shake hands with the individual.) "I work with Sally."
"Hi, I am Kayla-Leah, my son is number thirteen. Who are you here to watch?"
"Hello, Kayla-Leah. I just started in public relations here, how about you?"

Introducing yourself first shows confidence and is a great way to break the ice.

If you are introducing two people whom you know but they are unfamiliar with each other, there is a certain order you ought to follow to be in line with social etiquette. You begin by saying the name of the person who has a higher rank, or the person you wish to honor first. For example, if you were introducing your friend to your boss you would begin with introducing your boss to your friend.

"Bill, I would like to introduce you to my boyfriend, Sam. Sam, this is my boss, Bill."

To help myself remember this order, I just tell myself the first name out of my mouth needs to be the person of honor first. Here are some other examples of whom you would start with: adult, then child; woman, then man; guest of honor, then others: anyone with a title, then your friend; your client, then those in your company; grandparent, then friends.

One thing I frequently do when introducing two people is tell them a little information about the other; this gives me an opportunity to honor both parties while offering them a conversation starter. For example, I would say,

"Megan Bryant, this is my friend, Sally Smith. Megan was just nominated as Idaho's Woman of the Year and is the director of a comedy festival. Sally is a Hula Hoop Instructor."

Another polite social habit is to introduce a new-comer to the topic of discussion in a conversation. By quickly bringing them up to speed about what you are talking about the new-comer can join in, and you become a connector.

"Bill, we were just talking about the company party and who is catering."

Ask Questions.

People love to talk about themselves--it's in our nature! In a way, you can think of it as your job to get the conversation started. Ask the other person questions about themselves then use the answer to one question to prompt the next question. I guarantee if you ask questions about them, they will walk away thinking you are pretty amazing. It's a funny phenomenon, but it works. Then, you can use your next meeting as an opportunity for them to get to know you a little better.

Some questions you could ask are:
What do you enjoy doing when you are not working?
What type of work are you in?
Have you always lived in Idaho?
Do you like to travel?
Where have you traveled?
What types of hobbies do you enjoy?

You can use the situation you are in to prompt questions, as well. If you are at a party, consider asking them how they know the host. At a sporting event, ask about which athlete they are watching. Even in line at the craft store, ask what project they are working on. Be observant and use clues around you to start a conversation.

Why meet new people? I have heard that you become the average of the five people you spend the most time with. If you aspire to more than you are today, look around to others. Who would you like to be averaged with, whether it be your friends, mentors, or business associates? Find ways that you can interact with those you see living their lives similarly to where you want to go. A great way to do this is to volunteer where those people are volunteering; service opens opportunities to connect. Introduce yourself, start a conversation, and ask questions--you may be surprised when you have made a new friend.

A word on Bullies and Belonging.

Bullies can't always be avoided. We find them in nearly every social situation. Junior high and high school are probably infected the most, but bullying can be found in places of employment, neighborhoods, and even church environments.

Confidence is a great defense against bullies. Love yourself enough for everyone, even for a bully, love yourself in spite of anything a bully may throw your way. But bullying and harassment are very difficult to face day-in and day-out. It can chip away at your self-esteem and leave you feeling empty.

If I was to give any advice to someone who struggles with feeling like they don't fit in, or even how to counter-act a bully, I would suggest that they find somewhere where they feel a sense of belonging. If they can have at least one foothold in a place they are loved, respected, or valued, it can help with the struggle they feel in the places where they are not.

In high school, I was fixated on popularity. Although I had many acquaintances and many people knew my name, I felt lonely and unpopular. I would eat lunch by myself every day. However, on the weekends, I would go to debate tournaments. Some may have called me a debate nerd--I am fine with that! At least I was captain of the debate nerds! (Of course, you know I jest about the nerd part...right?)

At debate tournaments, I would engage with people my age who did not know my social status at school. They didn't know I had no-name shoes in gym class, they hadn't witnessed that awkward phase in eighth grade when I chopped my hair off and got a perm. These new acquaintances valued what I brought to the table, my skills as a speaker and debater as well as my friendly, outgoing nature.

We would often participate in tournaments with several schools and the tournaments took place nearly every other weekend from September through May. Even though I did not feel part of the "in" crowd at school, I felt a sense of belonging among those in speech and debate from other schools.

We all want a sense of belonging. So, my advice would be to find somewhere to belong. You can find belonging through service, hobbies, church, or clubs. Thanks to the Internet, more than ever before it can be simple to locate groups of people who gather with common interest. This will require that you move out of your comfort zone and into growth zone, and it may require you to meet new people. However, when you find a group in which you can belong, your confidence can grow immeasurably.

In Other(s) Words

"Be genuinely interested in everyone you meet and everyone you meet will be genuinely interested in you."
— Rasheed Ogunlaru

"Do not neglect to show hospitality to strangers, for by doing that some have entertained angels without knowing it."
--Anonymous

"Meeting a stranger can be totally fleeting and meaningless, for example, unless you enter the individual's world by finding out at least one thing that is meaningful to his or her life and exchange at least one genuine feeling. Tuning in to others is a circular flow: you send yourself out toward people; you receive them as they respond to you."
— Deepak Chopra

"If only you could sense how important you are to the lives of those you meet; how important you can be to people you may never even dream of. There is something of yourself that you leave at every meeting with another person."
-- Fred Rogers

"You are the average of the five people you spend the most time with."
- Jim Rohn

"We can never get a re-creation of community and heal our society without giving our citizens a sense of belonging."
- Patch Adams

Ed(you)cation

Make an effort to speak to three people this week that are strangers to you. Record what you learned about them and record what you learned about you.

Consider some of the places where you "belong." Do you need to find a sense of belonging?

What groups could you look into to gain a sense of belonging?

JOURNAL

"A bad attitude is like a dirty diaper, life stinks until it's changed."
— Orrin Woodward

WATCH YOUR ATTITUDE

I think every good teenager has been told at least once they need to "watch their attitude." I think the "attitude problem" often associated with adolescents comes with the territory of making life changes amidst the fluctuation of hormones. But there is something to be said about stopping and considering what type of attitude we have, no matter what life stage we're experiencing. Do we have thought processes that are optimistic or pessimistic? Focused on abundance or scarcity? Are we grateful or entitled, or do we see ourselves as the victim or the survivor (just to name a few)?

I hear negative attitudes around me all the time. I know negativity is a trap that is so easy for any of us to slip into. Negative thought patterns have a way of making it difficult for us to see anything in a positive light.

Many people feel victimized by coworkers, strangers, or people they are in relationships with. Individuals with a victim mentality feel as though everything negative happens to them, that they're magnets for misfortune and they have no control over having a more positive life.

So many people around us can only see what they lack; they lack a nicer car, a more lucrative job, a more dedicated spouse, a fitter body, a better life.

Too many are living in a space of scarcity. Scarcity is a land where jealousy, envy, and competition live. In Scarcity, you let others' successes take away from your abilities. Where you scratch and claw to get your "fair" share. Where you hold on to everything you have in case more is not on its way.

Sometimes we don't realize that we have been infected with a negative attitude. We can be oblivious to the negative thoughts showing up in how we speak and how we act. Often, it's easier for others to see our negativity than it is to see it within ourselves--our bad attitudes tend to hide in our blind spots. Just like our cars, we need mirrors to see these blind spots, angled just right to see the things we would otherwise miss.

How do we find these mirrors to see our blind spots? We could ask others who are close to us to see if we have a bad attitude, but their honesty could be hard to take. It can feel an awful lot like changing lanes only to find there indeed was a car in our blind spot.

We can self-diagnose by making a concentrated effort to pay attention to our language and feelings and evaluating what we hear and feel to see if indeed we have negativity looming in our habits.

Language.

Pay attention to your language. Negativity can be heard by using limiting language. Words such as always, never, can't, won't, and will are examples of language that give us a clue that we have already made up our minds about what is going to happen, limiting the potential for something to be anything other than how we've pigeon-holed it.

Here are some examples of limiting language with a pessimistic attitude:

"I am always late for work."
"I can never catch a break."
"I can't read long books."
"She won't follow through."
"I bet she will get sick."

The following examples use the same language, but coupled with an optimistic attitude:

"I am always picked for special projects."
"I never get sick."
"I can't see any reason why I couldn't earn the trip."
"I won't be in last place."
"I will get the job."

When you prematurely make up your mind about what you believe will happen in a given situation, then everything in your body will do its best to make you right. Have you ever heard of self-fulfilling prophecy? Our thoughts are powerful--we can be as happy or as successful as we make up our minds to be. Likewise, we can also be as miserable and misfortunate as we make up our minds to be.

As you pay attention to your language, what do you find? Have you predicted that something always has been or always will be negative? Or does your language show you predict something always has been or always will be something positive?

If you reflect on your feelings, do you find you feel hopeless, stuck, or limited? Like you are taking two steps forward then three steps back? These feelings can be an indication a negative attitude.

Changing our language will help us reshape our attitudes. When we discussed Words Matter in Chapter 5, several suggestions illustrated how we could turn around negative language to be more positive. Changing our language is a great place to start when we want to get rid of the negative attitudes that plague us! I want you to learn to tap into the underlying beliefs and attitudes that are hiding beneath your words.

Some suggested techniques for addressing the roots of a negative attitude:

Keep a Gratitude Journal.

A gratitude journal can be an excellent way to recognize the blessings you enjoy instead of focusing on what you feel you are entitled to or what you believe you lack. My humanitarian service trips to Haiti have taught me so much about needs versus wants, necessities versus luxuries. Seeing poverty on such an immense scale forced me evaluate, to my very core, what is needful for living.

After volunteering in the medical clinics, I could see that having enough nutritious food to sustain your life and health is a necessity. Clean water is vital. However, it isn't a need to have it delivered to the pipes in your home. As long as you have access to clean water, your water needs are met.

Having shelter is a necessity, one that can protect from storms like hurricanes. But very few things within that shelter are needs. I learned in Haiti that chairs are a luxury. Think about it--we don't need chairs. We can sit the floor. We don't NEED chairs. Turns out, flooring is a luxury too. Electricity--a bonus luxury! To actually survive, we need so few things. Everything beyond the essentials is extra.

We are so far removed from living for basic survival that we don't see the huge blessings of abundance, luxury and convenience that surround us. More than one set of clothing, clothing that actually fits. Shoes that fit. A bed. Any means of transportation beyond our feet, even a bike, is abundant.

If you keep your journal in attempt to see life through new eyes of gratitude, you will stop seeing all the things that you lack and you will begin to recognize the abundance you already possess.

Keep your gratitude journal any way you would like. Maybe it is on-the-spot journaling where you write it down as soon as you feel gratitude for something. Perhaps you strive to acknowledge a certain number of blessings each day. Maybe you will attempt to write one paragraph on something you are grateful for and why, adding how the blessing affects your life.

Benefit of the Doubt Game.

You only need to know one simple rule to play this game: give your friends, family members, and even total strangers the benefit of doubting that they intended harm when something negative happens to you. Instead of getting angry or frustrated when you interact with others, play the Benefit of the Doubt game.

Did someone cut you off in traffic? Stop! Don't respond with negativity--try to imagine a scenario in which the person cutting you off was the right move instead of the wrong one. The very act of this game will help change your attitude.

For example, think to yourself:

That fellow in the red VW, who just cut me off, is a skilled surgeon and has been called in to do emergency surgery that only he is qualified to perform on Benedict Cumberbatch. No, he shouldn't have had to cut me off. But, had we known why he was in such a hurry, all of the other vehicles would have have gladly moved to the shoulder.

Use your imagination, use your sense of humor, use any other muscle besides negativity. No, this game isn't going to change the fact that the guy cut you off, but it will change your attitude about it. Which is the whole point of the exercise.

Next, you'll learn about the opposite of The Benefit of the Doubt, and that is Assumptions.

Identify Assumptions.

I have always heard that when we ASSUME, it just makes an ASS out of U and ME. Assuming someone means to hurt, damage, or make us angry is actually a symptom of having a negative attitude. We take limited, and often skewed, information and fill in the blanks with negativity.

You see your two besties on Facebook checking in at the movie theater. They went to the movie without you! You assume that they chose to exclude you and then intentionally posted pictures on the Internet of them enjoying the movie together just to make you jealous. Your mind runs wild wondering why they don't want to include you anymore, and you wonder how often they get together without you.

Or, you can STOP and realize you have formed an assumption.

Investigating the facts vs. forming an assumption:

Fact:
Two friends posted a picture of themselves at the movies.
Assumptions:
How they decided to go to the movies together.
How they felt about going together instead of inviting you.
Why they posted a picture on the internet.
How often they get together without you

You may find out later that your two friends did not conspire to go to the movie together and purposefully exclude you. Maybe one went with her boyfriend, the other with her mom. While they were finding their seats, they discovered they were sitting on the same row. They took a second to sit next to each other and post a picture to Facebook to document the fun coincidence. They even laughed and thought it would be funny if you were there too, as they scanned the audience for you.

Victim vs. Survivor.

We all know that we can't change anyone else but ourselves. We can't control someone else's actions; we can only control how we respond to them. (Even though we know this, sometimes we forget.) We become victims when we focus on what others are doing instead of focusing on what we can do.

There may be many reasons we choose to be a victim in a given situation. Henrik Edberg, author of The Positivity Blog, suggests that we choose to be a victim because of the benefits.

He lists the benefits of playing the victim:
1. The attention and validation we receive from it.
2. We don't have to take risks (we stay in comfort zone instead of exploring our growth zone).
3. We don't have to bear any responsibility if it is someone else's fault.

172

4. It makes us feel right--like capital "R" right (no one likes to be wrong). (11)

There are times when people make really bad choices, and those choices have an effect on us. Sometimes we have played a part in the situation, but sometimes we have been innocently impacted. You can tell when you switch to a victim mentality when you focus your language on what "he," "she," or "they" said or did.

See if you can hear the victim mentality in these statements:

"He hasn't paid child support in months."
"They cut my hours at work. Now I am going to have to eat ramen because of them."
"My teacher moved our final up a week--she is so unfair."
"It's one thing after another. First my car, then my dog--life* is out to get me."

*(sometimes "life" becomes the "he," "she," or "they")

When you catch yourself complaining about he, she, or they, you can shed the victim mentality by creating a nevertheless statement for yourself. Or nevertheless can be implied, where it is just a pause or a comma. But nevertheless transforms us from the victim to the survivor.

See how nevertheless transitions the focus from what we can't control and gives us power to do something with our circumstances:

"He hasn't paid child support in months, nevertheless, I am resourceful and can make this budget work!"

"They cut my hours at work, (nevertheless) it looks like I need to up my game to show them I am worth the full-time position."

"My teacher moved our final up a week, nevertheless, it looks like I need to skip the open gym and study. Can you help me go over my vocabulary?"

"It's one thing after another. First my car, then my dog. (Nevertheless) it's a good thing I am strong enough to handle these challenges."

173

I know when unpleasant things happen you can experience shock, and there is nothing wrong with expressing your feelings and frustration about someone else's actions and how their choices affect you. What is problematic, however, is the overall attitude we embrace when we get stuck in victim mode. Where you heap in a big pile a list of all the ways you have been wronged. Where you share your story of victimization over and over and over with everyone you meet. If you want to change your attitude, focus your energy on what you can control and let go of the things you cannot.

Jealousy, Envy, and Success.

I am not sure I know anyone who likes to admit they were jealous of someone else. Jealousy isn't something most people are proud of and own up to. Jealousy can lurk in our blind spot as well, but fortunately it can be eliminated as we pay attention to our envious thoughts and the language they produce.

Envy doesn't have to be exclusively associated with material wealth. We can be jealous of others' positions, talents, accomplishments, the number of likes or shares on Facebook, blog followers, or their ability to leap tall buildings in a single bound.

Envy takes the stage when we feel there is limited supply of something (talent, money, time--take your pick!) and someone else has just cornered the market, not leaving enough for us.

One big symptom of envy is criticism.

"What makes them so special?"
"I could do better!"

Criticizing others is easy and offers us a false security; the underlying root of the problem has everything to do with self-criticism, the awful way we feel about ourselves which we project onto others.

Envy can show its ugly head at any age or stage in our lives. Envy can be pretty revealing about what advancements and setbacks we are dealing with in our own journey through our growth zone.

Maybe someone you know has pursued their dreams with vigor and success and you feel stuck in the "someday" phase. Perhaps this person seems to be zipping down the road at top speed while you feel like you are only idling. They have broken down difficult barriers while you're scratching your head and deciding whether to go under, over, or around them. You have taken the measuring stick of what you value and have applied it to others, and you feel like you haven't measured up while they have somehow managed to reach the top.

We are not often envious of the success of others in areas of life that are not important to us. I am not jealous of the title holder of the world's longest beard or the champion of downing the most hot dogs at a single sitting. When the success is in the same arena of our desires, however, then we can be more prone to becoming envious.

If you find yourself being critical of someone in your life, it might be an excellent opportunity to discover why you are feeling critical or invidious. What beliefs do you have that may have created these feelings of covetousness? Typically, the answers we discover are only about us and not the other person at all.

- Do you feel like you are not good enough?
- Are others doing what you want to be doing?
- Do you feel like there isn't room enough for you?
- Are you feeling stuck or frustrated in some areas of your life?

Recognizing your envy may be the signpost you need to point you in a new direction, a change of belief. Although the reasons may be varied, pondering on the why behind jealousy and envy can be beneficial.

There is enough (talent, money, time, etc.) to go around. Multiple voices are needed to share the same message, each in its own unique way. If someone has smashed through one of your stumbling blocks, then come to a space where you can ask for direction and seek help. Become inspired by the accomplishments of others. Let them motivate and challenge you in the most positive way.

Rejoicing in another's victories can actually propel you towards your own success. Happiness for others opens you up to abundance,

175

creating a synergy among others that allows knowledge and triumph to come into your life.

If you notice feelings of envy, stop and ask yourself what those feelings are really about.

Success isn't an exclusive club; anyone can join. The price of admission isn't envy, but self-discovery.

The path to overcoming each negative attitude is to look at the adversity you face in a different way. Redirect and channel your thoughts to something more positive; view yourself as an active player in a better outcome. In addition to the suggestions above, I want you to make a concentrated effort to seek out good books, documentaries, and even mentors to help you change the underlying issue of how you see the world and your ability to affect positive change within it.

A positive attitude becomes a bridge that can help you traverse even the most difficult situation. Build the bridge of a positive attitude by journaling, giving the benefit of the doubt, clarifying assumptions vs. facts, and redirecting your thoughts on things that you can change.

Helping Others

If you have a co-worker, family member, or friend who has a bad attitude sitting in their blind spot, I suggest you don't come right out and tell them their attitude stinks. I do suggest, on the other hand, that you evaluate your relationship with them to see if you are a safe person for them to receive feedback from. Start by sharing any articles or quotes you read about attitude. If you do feel the need to tell them, it is best to ask permission first. It can look a little something like this: "Would you mind if I told you something that I have observed about you?" If they say yes, be gentle.

"I have noticed that sometimes you tend to see yourself as powerless in X situation. I know that focusing on what you do have control over makes all the difference."

"I notice that you tend to be critical of Susie. Sometimes our criticism comes from others having opportunities that we want for ourselves. Have you considered that this may be he case with you?"

Keep in mind, some people will not yet ready for a blind spot mirror. Even if they gave you permission to share, they may not be happy with what they hear. Always follow up with love and acceptance afterward. Anything that tastes like criticism can be hard to swallow.

In Other(s) Words

"Your attitude can either be your best friend who has your best interest at heart or your worst enemy who wants to see you fail, destroy your life, and be miserably unhappy. It's imperative that you check your attitude. Make sure that your attitude is working for you, not against you. There's limitless value in having a positive, empowered, and optimistic attitude! Choose wisely which attitude you give life to."
— Stephanie Lahart

"If it's never our fault, we can't take responsibility for it. If we can't take responsibility for it, we'll always be its victim."
-- Richard Bach

"Today is a new day. Don't let your history interfere with your destiny! Let today be the day you stop being a victim of your circumstances and start taking action towards the life you want. You have the power and the time to shape your life. Break free from the poisonous victim mentality and embrace the truth of your greatness. You were not meant for a mundane or mediocre life!"
— Steve Maraboli

"Life is not compassionate towards victims. The trick is not to see yourself as one. It's never too late! I know I've felt like the victim in various situations in my life, but, it's never too late for me to realize that it's my responsibility to stand on victorious ground and know that whatever it is I'm experiencing or going through, those are just the clouds rolling by while I stand here on the top of this mountain! This mountain called Victory! The clouds will come and the clouds will go, but the truth is that I'm high up here on this mountaintop that reaches into the sky! I am a victor. I didn't climb up the mountain, I was born on top of it!"
— C. JoyBell C.

"If you don't like something, change it. If you can't change it, change your attitude."
- Maya Angelou

"Nothing can stop the man with the right mental attitude from achieving his goal; nothing on earth can help the man with the wrong mental attitude."
- Thomas Jefferson

"Often those that criticize others reveal what he himself lacks."
— Shannon L. Alder

"Abundance is not something we acquire. It is something we tune into."
- Wayne Dyer

"Gratitude unlocks the fullness of life. It turns what we have into enough, and more. It turns denial into acceptance, chaos to order, confusion to clarity. It can turn a meal into a feast, a house into a home, a stranger into a friend."
- Melody Beattie

"Every day we have plenty of opportunities to get angry, stressed or offended. But what you're doing when you indulge these negative emotions is giving something outside yourself power over your happiness. You can choose to not let little things upset you."
-Joel Osteen

"Assumptions are dangerous things to make, and like all dangerous things to make -- bombs, for instance, or strawberry shortcake -- if you make even the tiniest mistake you can find yourself in terrible trouble. Making assumptions simply means believing things are a certain way with little or no evidence that shows you are correct, and you can see at once how this can lead to terrible trouble. For instance, one morning you might wake up and make the assumption that your bed was in the same place that it always was, even though you would have no real

evidence that this was so. But when you got out of your bed, you might discover that it had floated out to sea, and now you would be in terrible trouble all because of the incorrect assumption that you'd made. You can see that it is better not to make too many assumptions, particularly in the morning."
— Lemony Snicket

Ed(you)cation

Pick one of the activities from above and focus on your words and thoughts to see if you need an attitude adjustment.

JOURNAL

SUMMARY

Dear reader. Dear fellow traveler. Dear friend.

No one wins when you shrink. The world loses out on the awesomeness of you. You miss out on an abundant Joy filled life.

I think writing a book should feel like taking part of your soul and giving it to the world. That's how writing this book has felt like it to me--I have tried to give you part of my soul, the part that aches for you to see yourself as you really are, to see your potential, your gifts, your uniqueness. I hope that in sharing with you some of the practices that I have used to help others develop and maintain confidence you were able to expand your own.

Through your Ed(you)cation, I hope you have learned to:
- know yourself, to love yourself.
- love yourself enough for everyone.
- find your purple crayons by asking "does it spark joy"?
- eliminate the gray crayon practices in your life with "or".
- break up with your inner voice bully.
- speak to yourself with positive words.
- visit the past with "nevertheless".
- create a vision for your future.
- be selectively vulnerable to slay your shame.
- dance with your fear by focusing on your "why".
- fill your bucket through service, smiles, and connection.
- meet new people and find belonging.
- feel empowered by keeping self-promises.
- apologize when necessary, and be grateful for lessons learned.
- focus on what you can do instead of what others do.
- cultivate an attitude of gratitude and abundance.
- give others the benefit of the doubt.
- pay attention to your language.

And don't even get me started on "beauty!"

My hope is for you to find that it is Fun To be You with Purple Crayon Confidence! I hope you tackle your life's journey with your shoulders back, your head held high, a smile on your face, and a twinkle in your eye. May you start each new challenge and adventure with your soul filled with possibilities, growth, fulfillment, and joy.

These are my hopes for you. Let the world see you!
Kayla-Leah Rich

In Other(s) Words

"To be deeply loved, means a willingness to cut yourself wide open, exposing your vulnerabilities... hopes, hurts, fears and flaws. Hiding behind the highlight reel of who you are, is the real you and that person is just as worthy of love. There is nothing more terrifying or fulfilling, than complete love, it's worth the risk... reach for it."
— Jaeda DeWalt

"I wonder why it is that we so often imprison ourselves in the opinions of other people. There can be no punishment worse than conspiring in our own diminishment."
--Dawna Markova

"You gain strength, courage, and confidence by every experience in which you really stop to look fear in the face. You must do the thing which you think you cannot do."
–Eleanor Roosevelt

"To be yourself in a world that is constantly trying to make you something else is the greatest accomplishment."
-- Ralph Waldo Emerson

"If you hear a voice within you say 'you cannot paint,' then by all means paint, and that voice will be silenced."
-Vincent Van Gogh"

"You wouldn't worry so much about what others think of you if you realized how seldom they do."
-Eleanor Roosevelt

"Trust yourself. Create the kind of self that you will be happy to live with all your life. Make the most of yourself by fanning the tiny, inner sparks of possibility into flames of achievement."
-Golda Meir

"Argue for your limitations and, sure enough, they're yours."
--Richard Bach

"Confidence is a habit that can be developed by acting as if you already had the confidence you desire to have."
-- Brian Tracy

"Trust yourself. You know more than you think you do."
--Dr. Benjamin Spock

"Successful people have fear, successful people have doubts, and successful people have worries. They just don't let these feelings stop them."
-T. Harv Eker

"No one can make you feel inferior without your consent."
-Eleanor Roosevelt

"It is not the mountain we conquer, but ourselves."
--Sir Edmund Hillary

"Nothing can stop the man with the right mental attitude from achieving his goal; nothing on earth can help the man with the wrong mental attitude."
-- Thomas Jefferson

"Always remember you are braver than you believe, stronger than you seem, and smarter than you think."
-- Christopher Robin

"One important key to success is self-confidence. An important key to self-confidence is preparation."
--Arthur Ashe

"It is confidence in our bodies, minds, and spirits that allows us to keep looking for new adventures."
--Oprah Winfrey

"Be faithful to that which exists within yourself."
– André Gide

"It ain't what they call you, it's what you answer to."
– W.C. Fields

"There are days I drop words of comfort on myself like falling leaves and remember that it is enough to be taken care of by myself."
– Brian Andreas

"You learn who you are by unlearning who they taught you to be."
— Nikki Rowe

"Who looks outside, dreams; who looks inside, awakes."
– Carl Gustav Jung

BIBLIOGRAPHY

1. H. (2015, May 14). Jim Carrey's Commencement Speech - Full HD. Retrieved January 16, 2017, from https://www.youtube.com/watch?v=QtpN-kOu5X8

2. The Holy Bible: the New King James version. (1996). Nashville, TN: Broadman & Holman .

3. Williamson, M. (1992). A return to love: reflections on the principles of a Course in miracles. New York, NY: HarperCollins.

4. Gain Confidence and Create Habits. (n.d.). Retrieved January 16, 2017, from http://liveboldandbloom.com/

5. Seuss, Dr. (1990). Oh, the places you'll go! New York :Random House.

6. Moreo, J. (2013). Overcoming Cancer: a Journey of Faith. Cork: BookBaby.

7. https://my.liveyourtruth.com/dyt/home/

8. http://undergroundhealthreporter.com/duchenne-smile-benefits/

9. http://www.compatibilitycode.com/book-resources/personal-qualities-list/

10. (http://www.dictionary.com/browse/beautiful).

11. http://www.positivityblog.com/index.php/2009/10/09/how-to-break-out-of-a-victim-mentality-7-powerful-tips/

12. Rowe, N. (2013). Once a Girl, Now a Woman. Balboa Pr.

ABOUT THE AUTHOR

Kayla-Leah Rich is a powerhouse of ideas and experience. She is a speaker, coach, humanitarian and author.

Over the last twenty years, as a Master Teacher and Coach, Kayla-Leah has transformed lives through one-on-one coaching and workshops.

She runs a local chapter of "Days For Girls" making feminine hygiene kits for girls and women in developing nations.

Her experience includes being a general contractor, a founding board member of a charter school, a leader in a worldwide relief society, and an advocate for children. Kayla-Leah is a 2017 TEDx speaker.

She is a fiber artist, snowboarder, irresponsible reader, proficient Googler, and lover of potatoes. Kayla-Leah currently resides in Meridian, Idaho where she is the rock star wife to Jason Rich, and the mother to 4 incredibly active sons.

Made in the USA
San Bernardino, CA
05 April 2017